HOLDING *onto the* GOOD

HOLDING *onto the* GOOD

W. L. MEASE

Holding onto the Good is a memoir. It reflects the author's present recollections of experiences over time. Some names and characteristics have been changed, some events have been compressed, and some dialogue has been recreated.

Copyright 2019 by Wendy L. Mease
All rights reserved.

ISBN: 978-0-578-40284-0

No part of this book may be reproduced, scanned, stored in a retrieval system, or transmitted by any means without written permission of the author.

"I am not afraid—I was born to do this."

—Joan of Arc

For Jesus.

For my beloved Billy.

For my husband, Rod, my angel and soulmate: Thank you for all that you are and have been. Beau and I are so incredibly lucky to have you in our lives and couldn't be more grateful for all you have done for us. I love our life together and look forward to continuing our spiritual path in this life. I'll love you for eternity.

For my son, Beau: You are my inspiration, and I am so proud of the young man you have become. I look forward to watching and cheering you on as your journey unfolds. Always know that I am so glad you are my son! Thank you for being you. My love for you is eternal.

ACKNOWLEDGMENTS

Thank you to Stormy, Billy, Mom, Grandpa, Gram, and Steph for being with me during this endeavor. It was more difficult to write than I anticipated. Nonetheless, it was a healing process. I miss you every second. Until our reunion, know that my love for all of you is with you every day and is eternal.

Thank you to my dear family for your encouragement and support, not only in writing this, but throughout the years. I love you with all of my heart.

Thank you to my great friends: Laura, Lisa, Sandy, Nancy, Beth, Theresa, Paulina, Nathan, Dean, and Kristen. I appreciate your friendship so much!

To my editor, Laura Matthews: Thank you. I couldn't have accomplished this without you! I am forever grateful.

Thank you to all of the musicians whose work continues to be an intricate part of healing in my life: Nickelback, Sade, Rascal Flatts, Bob Seeger, Lifehouse, Taylor Swift, Snow Patrol, Tony Carey, Ed Sheeran, Tim McGraw, Eva Cassidy, Carlos Santana, Cyndi Lauper, Dido, Josh Groban, Kansas, Kenny Chesney, Kenny Wayne Shepherd, One Republic, Randy Travis, Reba McEntire, Justin Timberlake, Sia, Sixx:A.M., Steve Winwood, T.I., Zac Brown Band, Rod Stewart, Sarah McLachlan, P.M. Dawn, Little Big Town, John Waite, Foreigner, Evanescence, Elton John, Counting Crows, Chantal Kreviazuk, Carrie Underwood, Bush, Blue Oyster Cult, Benjamin Orr, Blake Shelton, and so many more. Thank you for sharing your talents and the gift of music.

PRELUDE

I will try to tell my story as accurately as possible, but it's been a long journey so far and sometimes my memory is a little foggy. I should also say that, even though I relate memories here as I experienced them, I have forgiven everyone in my life who has ever wronged me or treated me with any unkindness. I can see it is all just part of my journey, and in the end, love is all that matters. This life is all about love, forgiveness, and always treating people with kindness. That was one thing that Mom always stressed to me and my sisters: Be kind to everyone.

I miss them all so much, those in my family who have departed from this life—my sister Stormy; my son Billy; my mom; my gram and grandpa; my sister Steph; and even my little baby girl who I never got to meet. There is not a day that goes by that I don't think of them. Remembering happier moments when we were all together and listening to music helps. I think of all our good times and how music was such a big part of our lives.

We always listened to music. I suppose we got that from Gram and Grandpa, since they always had music on in their house. They had one of those big, dark-wood cabinet stereos—the kind that had a record player in the center belly. You had to lift the wooden lid to open it. There were two speakers on both sides at the bottom covered with a gold, cloth-like mesh material. Gram always had the stereo polished so clean you could see your reflection. She always said, "We may not have the prettiest house, but we can have the cleanest." This planted itself inside of me at an early age, which would also explain my compulsion for cleanliness. My husband says you can eat off of the toilets in our house, they are so clean.

One of Grandpa's many favorite songs was "Shame on the Moon," by Bob Seeger. He told me when I was young that he thought there was a lot of truth to those words. That's when I started to pay more attention to the lyrics than the music.

As I sat and wrote my story, all my loved ones' favorite songs, along with my own, played in the background, from country, rap, pop, blues, soft rock—pretty much all types except bluegrass. Music was, and continues to be, a huge part of my life. I cherish the lyrics that have helped heal my heart. In an interview in January 2018, Reba McEntire said that, in times like these, music can be cathartic: "You sit down with a good album, a good piece of music, and it will heal your heart."

Every morning when I have my coffee, I tap on an application on my phone that gives me a random Bible passage for the day. Over the years, I have added my favorite quotes to a list. I've shared some of these with you, along with some beloved passages from books that are close to my heart. In one way or another, the ideas have given me strength and inspiration. I refer back to these often when I need a boost of faith. While I am not a religious fanatic, I consider myself to be very spiritual. My belief in angels and Jesus is the basis of my faith.

I hope my story doesn't evoke sadness, but it might. That is not my intention. I write this in the hopes of showing that faith in God's plan is so important. Everything is unfolding in life according to his divine plan, even though at times it is very hard to see or believe. There are days that I do question, "Why?" Nonetheless, this story is ultimately about faith.

I read once that fear and faith cannot exist in the same place at the same time; I hope that faith always prevails.

INTRODUCTION

I am no one special and am not a writer by trade; however, with the encouragement of my son and my friends who insisted that I tell my story—well, here it is. You will soon meet some of my family members who have passed: my sisters, my son, my mom, my grandparents, and my baby girl. In the midst of the losses, there are also battles with cancer—both my own and Mom's.

This has been a work in progress for over nine years, although I did not know it until I began compiling all of my journals and diaries after my son Beau left for college. Before my older son Billy's accident, I had kept daily journals and writings through the years documenting important dates, my thoughts and feelings of grief, and my struggle to find my faith again after losing it when Stormy died. It has been a journey—that's for sure. Sometimes it feels like I have lived many lives during this one lifetime.

In telling my story for my son Beau, it is my intention to show that through faith in Jesus Christ, our Lord and God, you can carry on no matter what may happen in life. I love Jesus with all of my heart and believe that I will see his plan when I am called home. What a reunion that will be! As Mom used to say, "Hold on, it's going to be a wild ride!"

CHAPTER 1

There are many rooms in my Father's house, and I am going to prepare a place for you. I would not tell you this if it were not so. And after I go and prepare a place for you, I will come back and take you to myself, so that you will be where I am.

—John 14:2–3

FEBRUARY 7, 2009

On February 7, 2009, I was at the urgent care center with my 10-year-old son Beau in Florida. He had bronchitis and a sinus infection. We had been up most of the night that Friday with his fever and coughing.

On Saturday morning, while we were in with the doctor, my mom called. I flipped my phone open, told her where we were and that I would call her back, and flipped the phone shut. She called again and again, but I didn't answer. I knew something was wrong, but couldn't think because I was so worried about Beau.

We left the urgent care center and headed to the pharmacy to pick up his medicines. As we got in line at the pharmacy drive-thru, I called Mom back. The first thing she said was, "Are you alone?" I said, "No." She asked if Beau was with me and I said, "Yes."

Mom said, "Hold onto him, Wendy. Hold on tight."

"What is wrong?" I asked, alarmed. I thought it might be Gram.

She said, "Oh, Wendy—Billy is gone!"

I screamed, "No!" I parked in a nearby lot and got out of the car to sit on the ground. I needed air. I asked, "What happened?"

Billy had fallen asleep driving to work early that morning in New Orleans for his job as utility company lineman. The highway patrol in Louisiana found out Billy's hometown was near St. Louis and had called the local sheriff to find his next of kin. Billy's paternal grandparents and a state trooper had come to give Mom the bad news. All of our families lived just outside of St. Louis in a relatively small town.

By now, poor sick Beau was beside me in the grass. I held onto him as Mom explained, "It was a car accident, that's all we know." Billy was just 20 years old.

* * *

For I am certain that nothing can separate us from his love: neither death nor life, neither angels nor other heavenly rulers or powers, neither the present nor the future, neither the world above nor the world below—there is nothing in all creation that will ever be able to separate us from the love of God which is ours through Christ Jesus our Lord.

—ROMANS 8:38–39

I drove us home, barely able to breathe. My heart broke into a million tiny pieces. I felt like I was turned inside out. Once home, I ran to the bathroom since I felt like I was going to vomit, but nothing came out because I hadn't eaten. I dry heaved into the toilet. It's a blur of events from then and for many more days to come. My whole world shattered. How I made it, I have no idea. My Billy. My Beau. My sons. My life. Billy was gone, and in an instant everything had changed.

Once I gained a little bit of composure, I got Beau settled as best as I could. I had to remember he had just lost his brother, and that he needed me to be strong. *How do I do this? Oh, my God, help me!* I didn't know what to do; I only knew that I needed help. I called my good friend Terry. She came right over, went to the pharmacy to pick up Beau's medicine, and made the plane reservations for me to fly from Florida up to St. Louis where all of our family was.

Beau was too sick to fly. I was torn; should I stay with him? Mom insisted I go ahead and fly up. Beau's dad could bring him in a few days when he was better. I called Jim (Beau's dad). I didn't want to call him—he had been so cruel to me since our divorce six months before—but I had no choice. He arrived to pick up Beau and actually hugged me. It was the first kind gesture he had shown me in years.

I remember thinking there was no way I could get through this, not with everything else that had happened recently—our ugly divorce, and I had just lost my grandpa, too. I had been in this situation 25 years before when my beloved sister Stormy was killed in a car accident similar to Billy's—in both cases, nobody saw the accident. Stormy was 19; Billy, 20. Both were illuminated souls who continued to make a difference even though they were not here any longer. My heart broke back then and was now even more broken. It will never be the same; nor will I.

* * *

He has brought us by faith into this experience of God's grace, in which we now live. And so we boast of the hope we have of sharing God's glory! We also boast of our troubles, because we know that trouble produces endurance, endurance brings God's approval, and his approval creates hope. This hope does not disappoint us, for God has poured out his love into our hearts by means of the Holy Spirit, who is God's gift to us.

—ROMANS 5:2–5

I wanted to go to New Orleans, where Billy's body was. I needed to see him, to be with him. He was there all alone. I wanted to go, but everyone told me not to; it could hold up the releasing of his body from the coroner. We wanted him back in Missouri as quickly as possible. I listened to my family. Part of me regrets this decision, but I also wonder what I could have done there. I could have been with him, or his body, but I also knew he wasn't "there."

I thought back to our last conversation, a few days before his accident. He talked about having a trailer hitch installed on his new black Silverado truck. He was so excited. He traveled as a lineman all over the country. He had purchased a big camper so he would always have a place to stay no matter where his work took him.

I reluctantly left Beau with Jim and went to Missouri. The trip was a complete blur. I don't remember flying from Fort Myers into Atlanta to my connecting flight or how I made it to the gate. I have no idea. I just remember watching my feet take steps and willing myself to walk. I asked God to please guide me because I couldn't.

I sat in the back of the plane and cried the entire way. There was a couple sitting across the aisle who kept looking at me, but I didn't care. I could not speak, I could not think; I could only cry. My head felt like it was spinning out of control. I asked God what I had done to deserve this. I thought I must have been a horrible person to have had so many awful things happen in my life. Before we landed, the lady across the aisle asked if I were okay. I told her I didn't think so and that my son just died. She said something like, "God is watching over you and your son," and handed me a little card.

* * *

The Lord is my shepherd; I
    have everything I need.
He lets me rest in fields of green grass and
    leads me to quiet pools of fresh water.
He gives me new strength.
He guides me in the right paths,
    as he has promised.
Even if I go through the deepest
    darkness, I will not be afraid,
    Lord, for you are with me.
Your shepherd's rod and staff protect me.
You prepare a banquet for me, where
    all my enemies can see me; you
    welcome me as an honored guest
    and fill my cup to the brim.
I know that your goodness and love will
    be with me all my life; and your house
    will be my home as long as I live.

—PSALM 23:1–6

Somehow, I made it and landed in St. Louis. I walked to meet my mom, my stepdad Dave, my sister Steph, and my stepbrother Luke (I consider him to be my brother and Dave to be my dad). When I saw them, I broke down all over again. Oh, my God, it was so hard! How was I going to get through this? *It cannot be real*, I told myself.

As my mom held me, I glanced up to see that the nice couple had followed me to my family, as if they were making sure I found them. I said a silent thank you to them. Days later, looking in my purse, I would find the card the lady had pressed into my hand on the plane. It was their contact information, like a business card. She had written on the back: "God loves you and will always watch over you." I think they may have been guardian angels. Thank you, God.

I don't remember much about that first night in Missouri at Mom's. I was a mess. I couldn't eat anything, and my eyes were swollen nearly shut from crying. I felt like I was in the middle of a nightmare. At any moment I would wake up and everything would be okay—right? But the aching in my heart reminded me it was real. Mom suggested that I have a glass of wine to settle my nerves since I was shaky and couldn't sleep. She poured me a glass of rich, red wine. It burned my stomach when it traveled down since I wasn't able to eat, but after a few sips, the alcohol started to sedate me. I slept fitfully, waking up several times in the night, reliving the nightmare of the day before.

I felt like I hadn't slept at all. I wanted to sleep and never wake up; or wake up and find it was all a bad nightmare; or wake up and be on the other side with Billy. And Stormy. And Grandpa. I didn't want to be there. I knew this was so wrong because I had Beau to take care of. I took a few Xanax that night—too many, I guess, because my mom couldn't wake me the next morning. Eventually, after the doctor reassured my family that I would be okay, they finally got me up that afternoon.

Billy's new camper arrived at his dad's house that day, and they invited us over to see it. It was much bigger than I had imagined it would be, but I thought it was just the right size for Billy. He never got to enjoy it. It made me sad to think of all of the things he would never get to experience. He had wanted to travel the world, especially to Alaska where he dreamed of living someday. I had asked him, "Why Alaska?" His reply was, "Because I imagine it is wild and free, like the last uncharted country." Billy never let any grass grow under his feet, as the saying goes. From the moment he was born, he was his own boss. Now, he would never marry, have children, and enjoy being a father and husband.

I remembered a conversation Billy and I had a few months prior—I had asked him if he was serious about the young woman he had been seeing. He told me not really.

I jokingly said, "Don't you want to get married and have kids someday?"

"Mommy," he said, "I'll never get married and have kids."

I now wondered if he knew somehow that he would leave this world early.

Billy's dad, stepmom, and I, along with my mom, met with the chapel directors. We went over what we needed to for the service, but I can't recall anything about the meeting. It still felt too unreal. It was pure hell to wait for Billy's body to get to Missouri—but then, so was every second of every day. Beau finally arrived with his dad the day before Billy's body, and we had a private family viewing on that Thursday evening.

* * *

Billy looked so good, like at any moment he could just open his eyes and be okay. Beau and I just stared at him; I could see Beau's little shoulders shaking. He stared at him like he was willing him to wake up. Billy was dressed in the clothes we picked out—a Buckle black and white button-down shirt with studs on it and blue jeans. His favorites. It was the hardest thing I had ever done to see him there. I told him I loved him so much. I kissed his sweet face. He was so cold!

I felt like my whole being was being ripped apart and my soul turned inside out. My thoughts were a jumble. I knew a part of me was gone forever. All I could do was to try to hold onto Beau, my wonderful youngest son, who was way too young to be experiencing this. It was so not fair!

Beau has always been such a kind soul. He and I each wrote a personal letter to Billy, to be placed in the casket. I told Beau to write whatever he wanted to say to his brother but didn't have the chance. It tore me up to see him now, looking at his brother, crying and wanting him to wake up as much as anyone else. God, I loved my boys! I would have done anything for either of them. I would have traded places with Billy in a second. It should have been me, not him!

FEBRUARY 13, 2009

The funeral was on February 13.

I remember the pastors saying several times during the funeral service: "This place." This place is where a part of my heart and soul will stay for a very long time, if not forever, or at least until we are reunited. It will reside in this place for as long as I am still here, until I am with him again. I can't wait; I don't want to. My heart ached so badly at the service, it felt like it was breaking into a million pieces. *This has to be a nightmare*, I thought. *It can't be happening*. But it was.

Hundreds of people came to pay their respects. I stood in the receiving line greeting everyone—friends, family, and so many other people. Some were crying softly, others sobbing. I just felt numb. When the pastors Don and Debbie began to speak, I remember them saying "this place" several times. It stuck in my mind. This place. This place. This place.

Mom wanted Don to read Psalm 27, as it was her favorite and she could recite it by heart.

> The Lord is my light and my salvation;
> I will fear no one.
> The Lord protects me from all danger;
> I will never be afraid.
>
> ...
>
> I will still trust God.
> I have asked the Lord for one thing;
> one thing only do I want;
> to live in the Lord's house all my life,
> to marvel there at his goodness,
> and to ask for his guidance.
> In times of trouble he will shelter me;
> he will keep me safe in his Temple
> and make me secure on a high rock.
>
> ...
>
> Teach me, Lord, what you want me to do,
> and lead me along a safe path.
>
> ...
>
> I know that I will live to see
> the Lord's goodness in this present life.
> Trust in the Lord.
> Have faith, do not despair.
> Trust in the Lord.

Before the service, we had decided that we would choose a song to play for Billy, one from me and one from his dad. I chose "The Only Promise That Remains" by Justin Timberlake and Reba McEntire. I chose that song because the only thing that really matters in this life is love. My love for my sweet Billy remained no matter what happened or where he was.

I believe that love is the basis and purpose of all life; we all strive to be loved, don't we? I think some people embrace this faster than others, and those who do not or who turn away from love contribute to the evil in this world. Those who understand and practice love cannot be involved in negativity—it is against the nature of love. Love transcends all else once fully realized by someone.

After the service, we went to the cemetery to place the casket. When we got there, I realized it overlooked the first little apartment Billy and I lived in after my divorce from his father, when Billy was around four years old. It was a little two-bedroom, one-bath government housing complex where they based your rent on your income.

We had so much fun there together, with many good memories even though I had little money. As I stood by Billy's casket, I could see the door to that apartment and the playground where we used to go. I could see me pushing him on the swing. We would sing together: "Swing, swing, swing so high, gonna catch a butterfly!" Only he would sing: "Thwing, thwing, thwing tho hi, gonna catch a buttafwy!"

I remembered how he loved to sit on the countertop in the kitchen, eating candy, singing Randy Travis's song, "Forever and Ever, Amen." That was his favorite song when he was little. I could picture in my mind the artwork that he and I had made together hanging on our little apartment walls—the only real decorations we had. I remembered how he loved to dress up like a ninja from Teenage Mutant Ninja Turtles, with his big brown eyes shining bright through the mask. Michelangelo was his favorite.

Before I was Billy's mom, I used to see young boys as they shopped with their moms at our local Walmart. The boys would wear mismatched sweats with their pants tucked into cowboy boots. I remember thinking, "I'll never let my boy dress like that to go to the store!" As Mom always told me, "Never say never," because sure enough, I often found myself at Walmart with Billy in his sweatpants tucked into his cowboy boots. I realized that as a mom, you do what you have to do to get to the store. It didn't really matter. After all, Billy was still my sweet son no matter how he was dressed.

As I remembered all this beside his casket, how I wished I could take back those moments now and cherish them. The tears streamed down my face. I always loved him so much! My sweet boy. How was I going to get through this? I had no idea.

Billy's senior picture, 2007

As for us, our life is like grass.
We grow and flourish like a wild flower;
then the wind blows on it, and it is gone—
no one sees it again.
But for those who honor the
    Lord, his love lasts forever,
and his goodness endures for all generations
of those who are true to his covenant
and who faithfully obey his commands.

                              —**PSALM 103:15–18**

CHAPTER 2

Your children are not your children.

They are sons and daughters of
   Life's longing for itself.

They come through you but not from you,

And though they are with you yet
   they belong not to you.

You may give them your love but
   not your thoughts,

For they have their own thoughts.

You may house their bodies but not their souls,

For their souls dwell in the house of
   tomorrow, which you cannot visit,
   not even in your dreams.

You may strive to be like them, but seek
   not to make them like you.

> For life goes not backward nor
> tarries with yesterday.
>
> You are the bows from which your children
> as living arrows are sent forth.
>
> The archer sees the mark upon the path of the
> infinite, and He bends you with His might
> that His arrows may go swift and far.
>
> Let your bending in the archer's
> hand be for gladness;
>
> For even as He loves the arrow that flies, so
> He loves also the bow that is stable.
>
> —**Kahlil Gibran**, *The Prophet*

During one of our last days in Missouri, Mom, Beau, and I went to Billy's dad's and stepmom's house to go through Billy's clothes and things. The five of us discovered that when Billy had needed to do laundry, he didn't. He just went to the local superstore and bought new socks and underwear. I chuckled silently through my tears saying to myself, *That was Billy—he never was into cleaning his clothes.* He would wear the same jeans for days and days, until I would sneak a wash in while he slept late. He would wake up and ask, "Why did you wash my jeans? They were just getting broken in and comfortable." He always had bigger and better things to do than worry about clean clothes.

We each kept a few of Billy's clothes and decided to donate the rest to local flood victims who had been displaced from rising river waters. Billy's suits went to a good friend of his who was about the same size. Beau asked if he could keep Billy's pool cues, and everyone agreed. Billy had been a good billiard player, and I had bought him two nice cues that he always played with. It hurt to look at the black cases sitting on the floor beside Billy's dog Jody, a big German Shepherd, as we finished dividing up his belongings.

Beau and I stayed at Mom's for six more days after the funeral, then flew back home. I wondered how I would go on. I knew I had to, but I didn't want to; I had to be strong now for Beau.

I felt like a stranger to myself—who was this person now? How would I support my son and myself when I didn't feel like doing anything at all? I couldn't feel anything, just numbness. I couldn't concentrate on anything; my heart hurt so badly that I thought it was going to fail. Sometimes, I couldn't breathe. I felt so alone. My friends said they didn't know how I was getting through this. I told them, "What choice do I have?" It was brutal.

I discovered there are certain things that should never be said to a newly grieving parent. Like, "At least you have Beau left," "Now he is in a better place," "You will get over this in time," " I know how you feel; my aunt just died last year," and "God must have needed another angel in heaven." Are you freaking kidding me? And, how do I answer the question, "How many children do you have?" I didn't know. I couldn't not include Billy, so at first I would answer, "Two, but one is in heaven." But, I found this usually caused people to feel uncomfortable and the conversation turned awkward. I decided to evade the question from then on. I was trying to survive. But it was not just about me; it was about Beau and my family and so many others who loved Billy. I got that. If not for Beau, I wouldn't have been here. I was there. Billy was not.

Billy touched so many people with his sweet mannerisms, contagious humor, and that laugh, along with his gorgeous, big brown eyes. When you looked into his eyes, it was almost like looking into heaven. They contained so much love and light. His soft, velvet voice became loud and boisterous when he got excited about something.

Would I ever get to gaze into those eyes again or see his smile? Would I ever get to hold him tight and tell him how much I love him? All those moments we shared together—gone. The fact that I didn't appreciate all of those little things compounded my grief. I had to believe that we would be together again. Hadn't I read so many books on the subject of life after death since my sister's death in 1984? Yes, I believe we will be together again. I feel it in my soul. The yearning for the reunion is the hardest, though.

Back at home, I struggled with the days and nights. Beau slept with me and woke up in the middle of every night, screaming for me. I knew he was having nightmares, but he didn't remember them in the morning. If he did, he didn't speak about them. We got up and got ready for school each day, and I held it all together until I dropped him off. I was not ready to go back to selling real estate yet. I couldn't do much of anything, but using my credit cards to pay bills would have to come to an end soon. Some days, I cried so hard that I didn't know how I made it back home after dropping Beau off—but I did. I crawled back into bed and cried. I woke up crying, and went to bed crying. Repeat. Repeat. Repeat.

* * *

Come to me, all of you who are tired from carrying heavy loads, and I will give you rest. Take my yoke and put it on you, and learn from me, because I am gentle and humble in spirit; and you will find rest. For the yoke I will give you is easy, and the load I will put on you is light.

—MATTHEW 11:28–30

Time passed slowly. I lived for Beau. Although I was not crying all day anymore, and I didn't cry in front of him as much, I felt it inside me all the time. I saved my tears for when he was at school, sleeping, or with his dad. On the evenings that he spent the night with his dad, I dwelled in darkness in my little rented house. I didn't want to watch television or read or do anything. Mostly, I listened to music quietly. I remember going into the master bathroom and staring at the large jetted tub, wishing I could take a long bath and let the hot water envelop me. I couldn't, because I didn't have the money to pay the water bill. I needed to save the space on my credit cards for food and necessities.

Instead, I wrapped myself in Beau's morning blanket (he always lay on the sofa with his cream colored velour blanket while he waited for me to fix his breakfast). I lay down in the bathtub and hugged the blanket all around me, taking in the sweet smell of Beau from earlier that morning. Sometimes I would fall asleep there and wake up in the middle of the night, not knowing where I was—until I remembered—and the sobbing returned along with the memory of what had happened. It was the worst feeling in the world. I was now a part of a group that I never signed up for—parents who have lost a child.

I was trying the best I could to be strong for Beau. It had only been a couple of weeks since Billy left this world. When friends asked me how I was doing, I would tell them I was fine. But I felt like some sort of freak, lying through my teeth. I wanted to say, "I am really struggling and don't think I can do this! I don't want to, and I am definitely not fine!" What good would it do to tell the truth, though? Nobody wanted to hear it.

I wondered how many people had felt the same when I had asked them, "How are you?" Now, I am more mindful when I ask people how they are doing. You never know what they are going through or the burdens they are shouldering. It made me more empathetic and sympathetic toward everyone around me.

The truth was, I missed Billy—his voice, his essence, his presence in this world. I missed his late-night phone calls, his texts, and the sweet way he said goodbye before we ended our calls. I just missed him!

Mom called me two or three times (sometimes more) each day. We stayed on the phone for long periods, sometimes not saying anything. Just knowing she was there gave me some comfort. I asked her, "How did you get through Stormy's death?" She told me, "You have to do this. You must be strong for Beau, and hold onto the good, Wendy. We don't and will not know the reasons why, but someday we will understand." She asked me to have faith, trust in the Lord, and talk to Jesus. She was my rock and my best friend, like she always had been my entire life.

I didn't remember how I dealt with Stormy's death because frankly I had blacked out the two years following her accident. I simply couldn't remember anything and still don't. I think I was too traumatized from losing her and everything else from my childhood. Beau forced me to be present following Billy's death. He needed me too much; he relied on what strength I had to get him through, just as Mom had done for me all those years ago.

I told myself that I needed to try to live in a way that would make Billy proud of me, but it was such a struggle. Beau was doing okay, most of the time. He had bad days; it came in waves for both of us. I felt so helpless because I couldn't give him any answers as to why this happened when I didn't understand it myself.

The Lord is compassionate, and when you cry to him for help, he will answer you. The Lord will make you go through hard times, but he himself will be there to teach you, and you will not have to search for him any more.

—ISAIAH 30:19–20

CHAPTER 3

You who do not see us, you who do not hear us, you imagine us in the far distance, yet we are so near. We are messengers who bring closeness to those who are distant. We are messengers who bring light to those who are in darkness. We are the ones who bring the Word to those who are in question.

—**Angel in the movie** *Faraway, So Close!*

Beau and I went to see a grief counselor once a week for about six weeks. I hoped she was helping Beau; it didn't help me or give me any ease. No one had the answers I was seeking. I turned to Jesus and the angels for help.

I talked to Jesus all the time. I thought of Mother Mary and the pain she must have endured while watching her beloved son suffer the way he did. My heart ached for her, and many nights I asked for her grace to get me through the nights and days. I became fascinated with all of the angels, especially archangels. I bought every angel book I could find and studied who the archangels were and what each one stood for.

For example, archangel Michael is the most powerful and represents protection, deliverance, and faith. He is also called the prince and commander of the angelic kingdom. Michael is the one I connect with the most. I learned that each archangel is also associated with a specific solar ray, sometimes called the seven rays of God's virtues and commonly known as a rainbow. These rays or colors are also connected to the chakra system in our bodies. The shades are blue, yellow, pink, white, green, ruby, and violet.

I read that each male archangel has a female complement alongside them. Archangel Michael's female counterpart is called archeia Faith. Together, they bring us the first solar ray, sapphire blue, which expresses God's power and will. This ray is found in the throat chakra.

The second ray, yellow/gold, is directed by archangel Jophiel and archeia Christine. The blended colors of gold and divine white represent wisdom and illumination and is found in the head chakra.

The third ray is pink and is associated with archangel Chamuel and archeia Charity who represent divine love. This solar ray is based in the heart chakra. Love conquers all!

Archangel Gabriel and archeia Hope represent the fourth white ray, which stands for hope, purity, resurrection, and ascension. All of the colors of the rainbow merge into this brilliant white light of pure divinity. It is found in the base of the spine chakra.

Archangel Raphael and archeia Mary govern the fifth ray, which embodies healing, truth, and concentration. This ray is emerald green and is associated with the third eye chakra. While Raphael is considered the great healer, Mary, the mother of Jesus, offers us grace, compassion, and mercy.

The ruby ray is the sixth solar ray and is found in the solar plexus chakra. Archangel Uriel and archeia Aurora bring us God's peace and teaches us to bring forth devotion. It is said that Uriel is the guardian of teachers and writers.

Violet is the seventh and final ray, represented by archangel Zadkiel and archeia Amethyst. It is associated with purification and transmutation by asking for God's powers of forgiveness, compassion, and freedom. This ray resides in the "seat of the soul" chakra just below the navel. It is known as the miracle of transformation ray.

I believe all of these angels, and many more, are here in our midst to support us and guide us all on our chosen paths, encouraging us to walk with love. We must ask them for their assistance, though. Believe me—I asked for their help every day.

Although I had no direct response, I started to feel and see them. I would see colorful little "orbs" throughout the house. These sparks of light looked like bright stars out of the top left corner of my vision. Once, when I was sick with the flu, as I lay on the couch I saw hundreds of angels all over my living room and kitchen. They were of all different, beautiful, luminous colors.

I started to collect every angel figurine or statue I could find. Since Billy's accident in 2009, I have now added hundreds of angels to both the inside and outside of our home.

* * *

The angel wearing linen clothes said, "At that time the great angel Michael, who guards your people, will appear. Then there will be a time of troubles, the worst since nations first came into existence. When that time comes, all the people of your nation whose names are written in God's book will be saved. Many of those who have already died will live again: some will enjoy eternal life, and some will suffer eternal disgrace. The wise leaders will shine with all the brightness of the sky. And those who have taught many people to do what is right will shine like the stars forever."

—DANIEL 12: 1–3

Mom and my brother Luke came to visit us for four days several weeks after we got home from the funeral. It was so comforting to have them with us. I felt so alone with no family in the area—it was just me and Beau. His dad lived nearby, but we were not on good terms since our divorce. One evening prior to Mom and Luke's visit, I was at Beau's baseball practice, sitting in my camp chair by myself watching the boys. Beau's father walked over and told me I had better suck it up or he would take Beau away from me. My jaw just dropped. I couldn't believe how cruel it was to say that. A part of me felt sorry for him for being so shallow. It reminded me of something in my past, from what seemed like a lifetime ago.

My mind drifted back to the abusive relationships I had been in when I was much younger. I was so grateful to be free of them now. Looking back, it's clear to see that both of my sisters and I continued the abusive relationships that we witnessed as we grew up. All three of us began relationships with men reflective of our own father. Unknowingly, we were continuing the pattern of being controlled by an overbearing male figure.

There were times that I didn't think I would escape those situations. I should have seen the warning signs when I was dating these men, but they had sucked me in with their charm and aloofness. They made me feel like they could "take it or leave it" as far as I was concerned; which only made me chase after them even harder.

By the time the verbal and mental abuse would begin, I was too far in to know what hit me. It started out slowly, in little things they would say or do that chiseled away my power, my self-confidence, and, ultimately, my self-worth. They told me that I wasn't "the greatest catch," that I was lucky to have them, that I walked funny. One of them made me call him "God," and if I didn't, I was punished with more verbal debasements. Nothing I did was ever good enough for them: I didn't make enough money, I wasn't frugal enough with money, and on and on. I was told to change my brown hair to blonde because it would make me look better.

By the time things would get physical, I was too worn down to do anything about it. One night, as I lay under one of them while he forced himself on me, I cried and begged him to stop. He just put his hand over my face to shut me up. I felt so degraded. When we went to see a counselor as a last-ditch effort to save the relationship, she asked him why he had forced himself on me. His reply was, "Because I felt like it." It made me sick to my stomach.

Mom was always my best friend. For that one, she asked me time and time again to leave. She said, "Wendy, don't you let him treat you like that. You have to get out of there." I was so scared to leave, since he had told me he would find me. Mom said I could move back home; she and Dave wouldn't let him hurt me. But I didn't want to be a burden to anyone.

I finally realized I was in the same situation Mom had been in with my dad. The cycle had repeated itself. As obvious at it probably would have looked to outside eyes, that was a revelation to me. I realized I did not want 17 years to go by stuck in the same bullshit Mom had put up with.

While this man was at work one day, I called Mom. I told her that I was packed and ready to go and asked if she could please come pick me up. She headed right over, but by the time she got there, he had unexpectedly come home.

He saw my suitcase and asked, "What the hell is going on here?" When I told him I was leaving, he said, "Like hell you are!" Mom came in and there was a lot of fighting, although I don't remember what was said. Mom got me in the car somehow, and, as we drove away, I saw him chasing us down the street in the rearview mirror. I would not return other than to pick up the rest of my things.

It had been so ugly that it took me a long time to realize how messed up I was. With time, as I lived with Mom and Dave, I began to get stronger with their support, love, and encouragement. Mom told me: "It is the weak who are cruel; gentleness can only be expected from the strong." She even taped that saying to the refrigerator so I would see it every day.

Where love is, God is. He that dwelleth in love dwelleth in God. God is love. Therefore *love*. Without distinction, without calculation, without procrastination, love. Lavish it upon the poor, where it is very easy; especially upon the rich, who often need it most; most of all upon your equals, where it is very difficult, and for whom perhaps we each do least of all.

—**HENRY DRUMMOND,**
The Greatest Thing in the World

CHAPTER 4

I am now giving you the choice between life and death, between God's blessing and God's curse, and I call heaven and earth to witness the choice you make. Choose life. Love the Lord your God, obey him and be faithful to him, and then you and your descendants will live long in the land that he promised to give your ancestors, Abraham, Isaac, and Jacob.

—**Deuteronomy 30:19–20**

About a month after Billy's accident, I eased back into selling real estate. I had no choice; I was sinking deeper into debt from paying bills with credit cards. I started working with a few customers and began showing homes in the area. Luckily, I had a few closings.

Seven weeks exactly after Billy's accident, I got a call from a friend asking if I would be open to meeting a great guy he knew. He said he thought I could use a friend. I said sure—but I wasn't sure.

His friend, Rod, called and asked if I would like to meet them for happy hour that Friday. I made the excuse that Beau had a baseball game. He called again. I declined. I told Mom I had no interest. She said, "Wendy, please go. I have a feeling about this guy."

Mom had not met Rod, but she always had a natural intuitiveness when it came to my sisters and me, so I listened to her. I met him for dinner that Saturday, March 28, 2009. I have no recollection of what we talked about, only that he was so kind and that his dark, almost black eyes were filled with compassion.

Beau was at his dad's for the weekend, so I was free to wallow in my grief. But Rod called the next morning. He said he was outside my door and didn't care if my eyes were swollen from crying or if I was a mess. I opened the door to find him there with a big bunch of flowers. I dried my eyes and got a vase, filled it with water, and put the flowers on the kitchen counter. He stayed all day.

We talked, although I don't remember what about. That night, before he left to go home, he asked if he could hold me. I said okay. For what seemed like hours, he held me and I could feel his warmth. It enveloped me, and I cried. No man had ever done that for me in my entire life. Rod was and is the kindest, the most gentle, yet the strongest person I have ever met.

* * *

So faith, hope, love abide, these three;
but the greatest of these is love.

—1 CORINTHIANS 13:13

The days went by, still in a dreamlike state for me. I felt like I was going through the motions of life but was not really present. I wished I could see Billy, talk to him, dream about him, anything! But nothing. I tried to stay busy with my work and Beau.

Rod started coming to Beau's baseball games with us. On one of the game days, I opened the front door to find him there smiling in a white button down shirt and blue jeans. Something hit me like a bolt of lightning—it was like I recognized him, finally, as my angel and soulmate. I had never experienced anything like it. I was mesmerized. We got in his car to go to the game, and Bob Seeger's "Hollywood Nights" began to play. I just kept looking over at Rod as we drove. He would glance back at me and smile. I felt my heart flutter, and there was a deep longing in the pit of my stomach. To this day, every time I hear that song I think of that day and can feel those same feelings.

Beau went home with his dad after the game, so we came back to my house. Rod was holding me on the couch. I had an overwhelming desire to let him know what happened to me earlier that day, but didn't know how to explain it and wondered if he would think I was weird. I simply said, "I haven't been with anyone in a very long time, but I would like to if you want." We made love then, for the first time, and it was like nothing I had ever experienced before. It was magical—no words can explain or describe it.

As the days went on, Rod would come over for dinner, and he would encourage us to try to see the good in life. He would open the blinds in my house and say, "Let God's light in!" (I had always kept the blinds closed because I wanted the house to stay dark since Billy's accident.) Slowly, the two of us became closer and closer, just as he and Beau were. He would tell me over and over how beautiful I was—something I hadn't heard in a very long time. He constantly complimented me on what I wore, or how I wore my hair, and did little things that began to make me feel better about myself. He took

Beau and me out for dinner, which was something I had not been able to afford. He took me shopping—I felt like Julia Roberts in *Pretty Woman*—and bought me so many nice new clothes. But it wasn't about all of those things. He was just so kind to Beau and me, and for that I was so grateful.

Rod and I were officially dating at this point. I had not realized it, but with Beau we were also bonding as a family. We played board games together, and Rod's antics and jokes made Beau and me laugh. It felt like we hadn't laughed in a very long time. We were actually having good times again. At first, I felt guilty for laughing, but then thought, *Billy would want me to laugh, wouldn't he? I know he wouldn't want me to be so sad.*

I could tell that Rod adored Beau. In our intimate conversations, he told me that he was so grateful to have me and Beau in his life—that he felt like it was a second chance for a family for him since his two sons left for another state with their mom after his divorce many years before. He didn't really get to be a big part of their lives. He did his best, though. When he told me this, I remember thinking how thoughtful that was of him—to allow his sons to go with their mom so she could live close to her parents for support.

There were rough times as we grew closer, though. Sometimes he became overwhelmed by my constant grief, and we would break up. He tried to help me but I was still helpless; I was trying but wasn't strong enough. Weeks would pass and I would miss him, but mourning would win over and overtake me. Somehow, though, he would get in touch with me and we would get back together. This happened many times. When we were apart, I would sink deeper into misery. I tried to be strong in front of Beau, but when I was alone it was pure hell.

Just before Mother's Day, Billy's dad phoned me to let me know that he had received all of the contents out of Billy's truck and that they had discovered two Mother's Day cards. He said he and Billy's stepmom read each one and had a feeling which one was meant for each of us. They mailed both cards to me and asked that I call them to let them know if I chose the same card.

Billy had never been the type to send me cards, but he always called me on my birthday, Mother's Day, and all of the other holidays, so I thought it was strange that he had purchased Mother's Day cards so far in advance. As I waited for them to arrive, I realized he must have bought them in January or February—that was doubly unusual. Where in the world did he find Mother's Day cards at that time of the year? Did he know he would be leaving this world and had planned ahead? It didn't make any sense to me.

I received the cards several days later. One had a funny cartoon while the other was more serious, saying how it made him happy to see his mom enjoying her life and trying to be happy, all of the things he had always wanted for me. My heart ached. I cried for my sweet son, who I missed so very badly. I called Billy's dad and we agreed on the cards—the serious one was for me. I told him I would send the other back to them for his stepmom to keep. He then told me that the funny cartoon card had special meaning for them. It was a little joke of some sort that only they knew about.

I wanted to think that this confirmed what I had suspected—maybe he did know something was about to happen to him. I kept asking God to show me any clues, even a sign or something—anything to answer my questions. As always, I was met with nothing but stillness. While there were no answers, I learned to be still and believe in faith.

Toward the end of May, Mom and Dave came down again for a week. They were worried about us being where we were with no other family, so Mom had been arranging for someone to visit us every few weeks or we would go up to St. Louis when we could. On this visit, Rod and I were back together and I was glad everyone was able to meet for the first time. They all got along great. Mom being Mom, she said to Rod, "You better be in this for the long haul!" He said he was. I felt relief. We got even closer after that.

Mid-summer, five months after Billy's accident, Beau's eleventh birthday was fast approaching. I didn't know what to do for his birthday. I wanted it to be a happy day for him. He told me he wanted to invite his friends from the baseball team over to our house for a party. He also told me that instead of gifts, he wanted to ask them to donate to Billy's scholarship fund that we had started. My eyes swelled with proud tears. What a great son I had! But I already knew that. I decorated the house inside and out, and the party turned out to be a great day. I thanked God.

Two days later, I would have my first dream of Billy. It was so surreal seeing him, I knew I had to begin a dream journal.

July 28, 2009

We were at a place with rooms; it looked like a chapel.

I went into a small room to find Billy laying on some sort of table. He had on his suit that he wore to Grandpa's funeral. I was alone with him and bent down to hold him. He said, "That tickles!" and smiled at me. I said, "Billy!" Instantly, he had on other clothes—jeans, shoes, and the turquoise shirt. I held him so hard and told him how much I loved him—forever and ever—and how much I missed him. He said, "I know, Mommy." (He always called me Mommy, even when he was 20.) He was sort of groggy; his eyes were glassy and seemed really sleepy. He was talking about his shoes and, I think, river water? He almost fell off of the table, and I yelled for Mom to please help me get him back up. I woke up.

I was so grateful to see him, and thanked God.

August 29, 2009

I dreamt about Billy! It's all in fragments. First, I was playing softball in high school, at a place that looked like my hometown, only bigger. Next, I was driving Gram around town; then, I was hanging out with Billy, only he was very young. Then, it fast forwarded to an 18-wheeler, where I was driving for Billy—it was his truck, I think. I got out of the truck to go inside this building. As I walked around the front of the cab, I saw him. I screamed, "Billy!" He looked so awesome; he was wearing a plaid Buckle shirt and jeans, and his hair was the same as it last had been—highlighted and long. He was so handsome! I smiled at him and ran to where he was standing. I couldn't wait to hold him, but when I got there he had vanished. I woke up crying. My heart ached.

Billy at Christmas, 2008

In September, I received a call that the headstone we had picked out for Billy's grave was ready. With school for Beau and work for me, we were unable to fly up to St. Louis to see it until Thanksgiving. Mom was on the phone with me and said she would take a picture of it, but asked that I not look at it until Rod was with me. I told her I would try to wait, but when I saw the email come in, I couldn't wait so I opened it.

It was beautiful but devastating to see. I still couldn't believe it was real. I was grateful we added an engraved carving of archangel Michael on the back. He reminded me of Billy—so fearless and so strong! I felt so close to archangel Michael and still do to this day.

I would dream about Billy again.

September 26, 2009

I dreamt of Billy! We were at the farm [my grandparent's farm—you will read more about their farm later], I think, but it looked a little different. He was in his truck, pulling a trailer. He was going to take it to his work site or something and asked if I would like to go with him. I wanted to go so badly but something or someone made me hesitate for a moment. I decided to go with him. He looked so good and so happy. He was dressed in dark dress pants. I knew what was going to happen next (the accident), and was very, very sad. I hugged him so tight and told him I loved him. I woke up crying.

October 10, 2009

I dreamt about Billy last night. We were at a big development, but it felt like the farm. Mom, Dave, Beau, Rod, and all of our family was there. I was serving others (there were other people there, too, but I didn't know them). Then, I saw him. I said, "Oh, Billy! You made it!" We hugged each other tight and laughed. Then, Mom, Luke, and I were at a table, talking and laughing. I went to go to the bathroom, and when I came out I was so glad to see he was still there.

Billy and I were getting ready to go somewhere, together. A song came on. I went to tell Billy I was ready to go. We ate shrimp at the top of some ladders. We climbed down and went to leave. The Snow Patrol song, "Chasing Cars," came on, only the words had changed to, "Woods road sold, show me your garden before it's too late."

I woke up and the alarm went off with seemingly the same song playing with the same changed words. I thought I was still dreaming. I wasn't sure if it was a message from Billy or Spirit and couldn't figure out what the words meant. As I laid there reliving the dream, I pictured what he looked like in it: so good and so very happy. His hair was shorter and back to dark, like it was in his senior picture. He had on the same shirt as in my last dream of him—the white button-down from Buckle. We were all so happy in the dream, laughing and playing cards. It was like we were in heaven, only at my grandparent's farm (or the farm was in heaven). I didn't know where Billy and I were going, but it felt like a good place. We were both content with leaving.

October 22, 2009

I dreamt about Billy last night! We were at the farm again, with the whole family there, inside the old farmhouse. It looked like it did when Gram and Grandpa lived there. I was talking on the phone with my brother Lucas, who was on his way there. I turned around and saw Billy in the kitchen. I screamed, dropped the phone, and ran to hug him. Billy turned to me and smiled. He was sluggish and heavy as I held him. He said he wanted to talk to me about the money. I said, "I know," and thanked him. He smiled. We fell to the floor, still hugging. I got up to do something, and when I turned back, he was gone. I began looking for him everywhere. I found him in Gram and Grandpa's old bedroom, only he was a little boy again, jumping on the bed with Lucas in their underwear, like they used to do when they were little. I smiled as I watched them play, then woke up.

When I went to make the bed that morning, a large white feather was under my bed. This was when I began to find feathers everywhere, even though I had no down pillows, comforters, or anything with feathers in the house. I knew they were from Billy. I started saving them by my bedside.

One morning, around 2:00 a.m., I came out to the kitchen because I couldn't sleep. As I rounded the bedroom door that leads to the kitchen, I saw life-sized white, almost glowing, angel wings rounding the corner as if the angel were trying to hide. I was not dreaming and I know what I saw. I offered a prayer of thanks to God and the angels, mainly archangel Michael for protecting us.

It was so surreal to dream about him. I was grateful to see him, but it also made me long to be with him. I knew it wasn't right to want to leave—that I had to be here. Mom kept telling me to "hold onto the good," to have faith in God's plan. We have to, she told me; that's the only thing that gave her strength. That, and our family. She said we have the best kids, and she was right.

We are always full of courage. We know that as long as we are at home in the body we are away from the Lord's home. For our life is a matter of faith, not of sight. We are full of courage and would much prefer to leave our home in the body and be at home with the Lord.

—2 CORINTHIANS 5:6–8

CHAPTER 5

Yes, it is God who raises the humble
and gives joy to all who mourn.

—Job 5:11

I was still not sleeping very much and had lost so much weight. I was down to 98 pounds, but I didn't care. I usually woke up between 1:30 and 3:00 a.m. Most of the time I would write, but I didn't know why. On one particular early morning, I sat down at the kitchen table and wrote something I know didn't come from me. I believe it was a message from Billy because as soon as I finished, my cell phone powered itself down and then back up again, right next to me. Here's what I wrote:

> Consider this: Sometimes when we let go, when we let someone we love so very much go and do what their soul needs to do or go where they need to, it brings them back to us, even closer than before. For as you let them go with love, willing to experience profound grief and pain for your loss (not theirs), as you have elevated their soul by your pure love, their soul does know this. Your relationship is also elevated to a new level of pure love, and nothing can ever break that. Not time, space, or even death. This holy, loving relationship lives forever. For as you truly let go with pure love, not even knowing the outcome, the heavens rejoice and God blesses.

After my hand finished writing, I went to make a cup of coffee and go outside to smoke a cigarette. I felt like I was glowing. It was strange, but in a good way. When I finished, I went inside and read what was written. Yes, I thought to myself, it was a sacred message. I felt the truth of it in the depths of my soul. I realized it was right but also knew how hard it was. I had to hold onto the good.

* * *

In this manner therefore pray ye:
Our Father, who art in Heaven,
    hallowed be Thy name.

Thy kingdom come. Thy will be done
    on earth, as it is in Heaven.

Give us this day our daily bread.

And forgive us our debts, as we
    forgive our debtors.

And lead us not into temptation,
    but deliver us from evil. For Thine
    is the kingdom, and the power
    and the glory forever. Amen.

—MATTHEW 6:9–13

November came and with it Billy's birthday and Thanksgiving. What do you do for your son on his birthday when he is not there? I felt an immense emptiness in my heart. I thought how hard it would be for Beau, so I needed to try and stay strong for him. Rod, Beau, and I decided to get a bunch of white balloons and take them to the beach. On Billy's birthday, November 12, 2009, we took 21 balloons to the beach; we said a prayer, wished him a happy birthday, then released them. Tears streamed down as I watched them float higher and higher until I could no longer see them. *Gone, just like him,* I thought to myself. I wanted to scream, "This is so hard! What can I do?"

The first Thanksgiving without Billy, Beau, Rod, and I flew up to St. Louis to be with the family. I don't remember anything about that trip, except for visiting Billy's grave with the new headstone. In the cold, damp, November weather, we drove up to the cemetery. There was a knot in my stomach tighter than I had ever felt, and I thought I was going to throw up. I told myself to stay strong for Beau. He was in the backseat looking out the window, and I knew, or felt, that he was feeling the same way as I was. Rod parked the car, and we all got out. I went to Beau and put my arm around him as we walked to Billy's grave.

When I saw the headstone, I lost it. I couldn't help it. I fell to the wet ground and cried like I did when I first learned of his accident. I cried so hard I couldn't breathe. I touched and kissed his headstone, on the picture of him that we had added. I told myself to pull it together. I got up and went to hold Beau. I told him I was so sorry. He said, "Me, too." We placed the flowers on the grave.

* * *

Your joy is your sorrow unmasked. ...
The deeper that sorrow carves into your
 being, the more joy you can contain. ...

When you are sorrowful look again
 in your heart, and you shall see that
 in truth you are weeping for that
 which has been your delight.

Some of you say, "Joy is greater than sorrow,"
 and others say, "Nay, sorrow is the greater."

But I say unto you, they are inseparable.

Together they come, and when one sits
 alone with you at your board, remember
 that the other is asleep upon your bed.

— **KAHLIL GIBRAN**, *The Prophet*

Back home, I felt myself sinking into a void of nothingness. The final thing to do for Billy had been his headstone. There was nothing left to do; all was done. December came and so did more dreams of Billy.

December 4, 2009

I was bear-hugging Billy in my dream last night. That's all I remember about him. Mom, Steph, and I were at the farm, which had a graveyard in the back. We were placing flowers on all the graves when wolves began coming down the hill. We went inside the barn that was now a house. The wolves were at the windows and doors, trying to get in. I woke up.

December 7, 2009

I dreamt I was receiving a message from God/Spirit. It was written in a holy book of some kind that was glowing. It said to me, "You must work through this; don't try to escape from it, it cannot be ignored. As you face it, truthfully, it will transform you."

Somehow, in my dream, I sensed that Billy likes the angel candles I burn for him and knows what I keep in my pocket every day.

In my pocket, I keep a coin that my sweet friend LB gave me after the funeral that says, "Gone yet not forgotten, although we are apart, your spirit lives within me, forever in my heart," and a coin of Mary Magdalene from the Vatican.

In my dream, I had heard music with bells in my right ear but I wasn't sure what song it was. When I woke up, my ears were ringing so loud I almost didn't hear the song that played by my bed: "By Your Side," by Sade. This was the same song I recognized that had been playing in my dream. Was this a message from Billy? I felt like Billy was letting me know that he was "taking care" of me from heaven, almost like he was singing the song to me. I wanted to think so and have cherished that song ever since.

December 23, 2009

In December, I phoned into a radio station hosting a psychic who was taking questions. I had tried to get through for the prior few months but never succeeded. I asked archangel Michael and Billy to please get me through on that particular day.

At first, I got the usual busy signal but decided to try again. This time, the DJ answered and told me I was the last caller. "What is your question for Psychic Mike?"

I asked if the new year would be better because the current year had been horrible. Mike said yes, but I was holding onto the past and needed to let go and clear out. I asked about Billy. He said, "Major blow to the head?" I said yes. Mike said he crossed over to heaven before he was killed so he didn't feel any pain, and that he immediately visited everyone once he realized he could go anywhere. He said I was the first person Billy visited and that he was with me every day and loved me very much. Without me asking him, he said Billy was the one who flicked the lights and left me the feathers. We hung up, and I said a prayer of thanks to archangel Michael and Billy.

Rod, Beau, and I flew up to St. Louis for Christmas. It was the first Christmas without Billy. It was so hard because I realized it would be the end of the first year of "firsts" since he passed, and that it would not be the last Christmas without him. I tried to be strong. I tried.

January, 2010

The new year came, and I began to sign up for floor duty at the office. Floor duty is a block of time at the real estate office where you assist people inquiring about available homes in the area or possibly listing their home for sale. Typically, it is a very boring time since we didn't have a lot of walk-in traffic.

My heart was not in it. I didn't want to do it anymore, but how was I going to support us? The real estate market was not good, especially for me since I had not done much the previous year. By the second week of January, I knew I had to do something else or lose my mind completely.

Rod, my angel, called the beginning of the third week to let me know an onsite position had opened up for a real estate developer selling new residences. He was friends with the broker and asked if I wanted him to make a call. I said yes, please! I got the job and started the last week of January.

Trust in the Lord with all your heart.
Never rely on what you think you know.
Remember the Lord in everything you
do, and he will show you the right way.

—**PROVERBS 3:5–6**

CHAPTER 6

And now I give you a new commandment: love one another. As I have loved you, so you must love one another. If you have love for one another, then everyone will know that you are my disciples.

—John 13:34–35

The new job was such a blessing in so many ways. First, it would make me get up, get dressed, and go to work. Second, it would mean more money. Third, it would be great experience.

I worked with JR and Dan, and we all shared what we sold. This worked out great. If any of us needed to take time off, we could do so without sacrificing commissions. JR and I became friends and spent our downtime at the office sipping coffee and joking. I realized I was getting stronger.

February 7 was approaching—the one-year anniversary of the worst day of my life. I wondered if I would be able to make it through the day and hide my pain and grief. Somehow, I believe by the grace of God, I made it. I went home and wrote my first letter to my son since his funeral.

> Dear Billy,
>
> I miss you so very much! Where are you? I know you are in heaven, but where is that? Are you with Stormy and Grandpa and the rest of our family? What is it like?
>
> There are so many things I want to say to you, so many things to tell you—where do I start? I miss talking to you. I want to hug you and tell you how much I love you. There are so many things left unsaid for me. I feel that maybe you know these things somehow, or maybe it's just me being hopeful in the midst of all of this heavy grief.
>
> If it is possible that you can see me here on this Earth, maybe you know all of this, how I am feeling, things that I am saying and not saying, and that sometimes I drink too much wine at night so I can sleep. I am trying to hold onto the good, like Mom tells me, and to stay connected to Jesus, God, and the angels. They are the source of what strength I have, and for this I am grateful. I have to believe that I will be with you again,

that someday all of us will be together again in the place where there is no pain, no grief—only peace and love.

Thank you for when you visit me in my dreams. I love seeing your beautiful eyes and that smile! I love you so very much! You are always in my heart, my sweet son.

All my love—eternally,

Mom

Beau had been reaching out to everything Billy had been into. I took him shopping at Billy's favorite store, Buckle, and bought him clothes that he picked out thinking Billy would like them. He played the music of Three Days Grace a lot. When he found out they were coming to Fort Myers for a concert, we got tickets. On the last Friday of that February, I took Beau to his first concert. There, I saw how he was in awe of the band. He was still a little boy, with so much to yet experience and see. I vowed to be a better mom.

By the second week of March, nearing the one-year anniversary of dating Rod on and off, I knew something was going on with my body. A pregnancy test confirmed what I suspected, and so did a visit to the doctor.

I was in shock. How could I raise this baby in the midst of all of this? Rod was excited, and I wanted to think that perhaps this baby would be a blessing—a new little soul to love and care for. I felt like it was going to be a girl for some reason and thought of a name: Bella.

But it was not be meant to be. Two weeks later, I lost the baby. Rod and I broke up because we were so devastated. My hormones were all out of whack; I was a mess. I worked, took care of Beau, and went through the days trying to put up a strong front. I missed Rod. I couldn't listen to music anymore. It used to be such a comfort to me. After this happened, music made me cry.

* * *

Those who trust in the Lord for help will find their strength renewed. They will rise on wings like eagles; they will run and not get weary; they will walk and not grow weak.

—ISAIAH 40:31

When I drove to work, I looked for Rod's car on the road. I still also looked everywhere for Billy, especially if I saw a black Silverado truck like he had. Now, I was looking for both of them. Was this the denial phase of grief? People had sent me books for grieving parents that described the phases. I eventually wanted to chuck them in the trash and scream, "There are no answers!" Instead, I kept them. They are tucked safely in the back of my closet where I can't see them.

Beau and I started to get used to life without Rod. We were coping. I knew Beau loved him too, so I stayed positive and strong when we were together. I had to, for him. I just felt so empty inside.

October 11, 2010

Among many vivid dreams last night, I dreamt I was in a glowing place. I saw hands that were surrounded by a bright light, holding a white dove. The hands turned to me, the dove looked at me, and then, the hands released the dove, and it flew directly into my head.

Beau and I went to St. Louis for Thanksgiving in 2010. The minute I saw Mom, I knew something was wrong. She was slurring words; her eyes were vacant and she was shuffling as she walked. I pleaded with her to call the doctor. She eventually made an appointment for January. I thought, *That is too far away*.

The first of December, my doctor asked me to come in for an ultrasound after a routine mammogram. I had been talking to Mom every day on the phone and had continued to notice by her voice that she was getting worse I didn't think anything further about the mammogram—I was too worried about Mom. I begged Dave and my sister to take her to the hospital, but Dave said she was just tired. Steph said she was doing fine. I called and made the appointment for my ultrasound on December 29th.

* * *

To have faith is to be sure of the things we hope for, to be certain of the things we cannot see.

—HEBREWS 11:1

I was in bed on the morning of December 26 and had an overwhelming itch on my breast bone. I began to itch it and felt a lump. I knew what it was. I needed Rod.

I contacted him and told him that I thought I had cancer. He came right over. When I explained that I didn't have the official diagnosis, he reassured me that it was not cancer and that I would be fine. While he was here at the house, I got a call from Dave. Mom had fallen in the shower, and they were at the hospital. He said, "I'm sorry to tell you this but your Mom has brain cancer. It has splintered throughout her brain. They are going to try to remove as much as they can tomorrow." I told Dave I would be on the next flight out. Looking back, I thank God that Rod was there. I would have been alone, since Beau was with his dad for that week.

I flew up to St. Louis the next day and went straight to the hospital. The whole family was there as well as some good friends. When I walked into the waiting room I broke down crying. I thought, *This can't be happening again!* Mom was out of surgery but was still in recovery, so no one had seen her yet. It was late, and everyone was exhausted.

I offered to stay the night and let them go home to get some rest. They gratefully accepted, and one by one started leaving to go home. Soon, it was just Dave and myself. As soon as we could, we were taken to see Mom. Her head was completely wrapped in gauze. Although she was sleeping, she opened her eyes for a moment and gave a little smile.

The doctor said they took a big portion of the cancer out, but they couldn't get it all as the tumors had splintered and woven around her brain. He said she could have a few months to live, or over one year. There was nothing further to do that night, he said, and we should go home and get some rest. I looked at Dave. He looked so tired. I assured him that I would be fine, and he went home.

* * *

Do not be afraid—I am with you! I am
your God—let nothing terrify you!
I will make you strong and help you;
I will protect you and save you.

—ISAIAH 41:10

I settled into the chair next to Mom's bed and watched as she slept peacefully. My sweet Mom. She didn't deserve this, not after all that she had endured. I prayed so hard to God, asking him to please heal her and to let her be okay.

While she slept, I cried. When she woke up, I held her hand and told her how much I loved her.

At that moment, she suddenly smiled a huge smile and said, "They are here!"

I asked, "Who?"

"I see Billy and Stormy! They are right beside you, Wendy!"

Tears of joy slid down her face. I knew this was the first time she had seen them since they both passed. I also knew that since Stormy's accident in 1984, Mom had never dreamed about her daughter. I realized how lucky I had been to dream about Billy so often.

Mom fell back to sleep. I didn't allow myself to sleep in case she woke up and needed anything. All I could do was sit and watch.

As the scripture says, "What no one ever saw or heard, what no one ever thought could happen, is the very thing God prepared for those who love him."

—1 CORINTHIANS 2:9

CHAPTER 7

Life is so generous a giver. But we, judging its gifts by their covering, cast them away as ugly or heavy or hard. Remove the covering, and you will find beneath it a living splendor, woven of love, by wisdom, with power.

Welcome it, grasp it, and you touch the angel's hand that brings it to you. Everything we call a trial, a sorrow, or a duty, believe me, that angel's hand is there.

—Fra Giovanni Giocondo

As I sat next to Mom in the hospital, my mind drifted back to my childhood.

I have blacked out much of my youth, probably for the sake of my sanity since many parts would be too traumatic to remember. I suppose this is a defense mechanism.

When I was a girl, my family lived in a very small rural farming town. Almost everybody was a farmer, and everyone knew everyone. Our house was on a farm of about 150 acres and had horses, pigs, dogs, cats, and cattle. My grandparents lived on the other side of a wildlife conservation area that sat in between our homes so we could ride our horses or motorcycles over to their house through the protected wildlife area.

My sisters Stormy and Stephanie and I were very close and as close to our mom as any children could be. Mom was our refuge and our rock since life in that house was not easy. Our father was a harsh and abusive alcoholic at times, while our mother was the most gentle and kind person I knew. When Dad was sober, he was a good man—fair to everyone, and he kept his word and guided us with a firm, loving hand. I don't believe Dad remembered being abusive since it only happened when he was so intoxicated. On the mornings after an ugly episode, he would act like nothing happened.

I learned at an early age not to speak about it. I suppose he couldn't help it since he was abused as a child, or so Mom told me. I don't remember Dad's parents; they passed when I was too young. Mom said Dad used to wake up in the middle of the night, screaming. As I said, I have completely forgiven my dad and have nothing but love for him; nonetheless, some of the memories still haunt me.

My first memory is of me hanging from the kitchen cabinet. I guess I had climbed up to get something off the counter. When I tried to jump down, my diaper got caught on the knob. I cried out, and Mom came running in. She started laughing as soon as she saw me, and she got me down to safety. I think I was around 2 or 3, but I'm not sure. Mom told me I started walking at 6 months old (we have pictures to prove it!) and rarely slept—I went to bed around midnight and woke up at 6:00 a.m.

I was a little hellion. Mom always said if I had been her first born, I would have been her last. She told me how she would find rabbit feet and squirrel tails, still with body parts attached, under my bed. I used to chase my sisters around the outside of the house with black snakes. I was so stubborn that I would only wear one outfit to kindergarten every day—brown pants and a navy blue T-shirt with a donkey baring its big teeth, saying, "Who cut the cheese?" It was my favorite.

I can still hear Mom telling me, "I hope you have a child just like you one day!" or "I brought you into this world and I can take you out of it!" But I knew she was joking. She would smile at me, then laugh.

Like a lot of youngsters, I was obsessed with farts. I used to make those similar sounds by cupping my hand in my armpit and pumping my arm up and down. I could also do it with the back of my knees. I thought I was brilliant, but Stormy would just roll her eyes.

* * *

I was fearless; there was nothing that I wouldn't do or try. One summer day I was out mowing the backyard and accidentally ran over the extension cord that was plugged into our pool pump. I shut the mower off and picked up the cord, wondering how I was going to fix this so Mom wouldn't find out. I promptly electrocuted myself, with black streaks going all of the way up my arms. Needless to say, that was the end of my mowing for a few years since Mom wouldn't let me near the mower after that.

Stormy and I had motorcycles that we bought from selling the pigs we had raised. Stormy's was a red and black Suzuki 125, and mine was a grey and black Suzuki 75. Steph was too little to drive, so she always rode behind me. Mom taught us to check the oil before each ride. I had to use a dipstick that Mom kept in a drawer in the kitchen. Stormy's dipstick was attached to her oil cap. Once, after we walked down to the little shed below our house where our motorcycles were stored, I said, "Oh shit, I forgot the dipstick!" Steph said, "No you didn't, I am right here!" My poor little sis—I used to call her a dipstick.

I loved to ride by myself so I could do stunts like Evel Knievel. I would go full-throttle down our gravel road, leaving a trail of dust behind me. One time, I decided to try to jump the gravel road—there were little banks on each side. I got ready to jump it, revved the engine, let out the clutch, roared up the bank, flew over the gravel road, and landed head first on the other side. It was such a rush, but I had totaled my motorcycle. I don't know how I didn't break my neck! That was a long time ago when I had a lot of "spit" about me. At least, that's the word Mom used. Many, many years later, after I left that abusive relationship, she used to tell me to "get your spit back."

We were lucky we had the freedom of living on the farm. We'd ride our bikes down to the creek, my sisters and I, and look for rocks, crawdads, and other creatures. We rode into town and bought one-cent Dubble Bubble gum and soda at the little grocery store. Mom used to take us fishing.

One of my favorite things to do was go horseback riding. Sometimes I would go by myself and would run one of my horses as fast as I could—I felt so free! My two favorite horses were a Palomino named Candy and a Pinto named Missy. They could gallop lightning fast. Some days, I would walk out to their pasture below our house and grab one of their manes, jump up, and take off riding bareback. Other times, my mom and sisters and I would go together, sometimes along with some of our neighbor friends. Summers were filled with working Mom's garden, canning vegetables for the winter, riding horses, three-wheelers, and motorcycles, playing softball, and spending time with Gram and Grandpa, whom I adored.

* * *

Me, Mom, Steph, and Stormy, 1978

For this reason we never become
 discouraged. Even though our
 physical being is gradually decaying,
 yet our spiritual being is renewed
 day after day. And this small and
 temporary trouble we suffer will bring
 us a tremendous and eternal glory,
 much greater than the trouble.
For we fix our attention, not on things that
 are seen, but on things that are unseen.
 What can be seen lasts only for a time,
 but what cannot be seen lasts forever.

—**2 CORINTHIANS 4:16–18**

I loved going to Gram and Grandpa's house—it always smelled of Gram's cooking. Whether it was her homemade yeast rolls, pot roasts, fried chicken, or cookies, it always smelled like home. Every Sunday after church, we all went to their house for a huge lunch, which always included those homemade rolls. Gram would scurry around her sunny, yellow kitchen in her apron, making the last preparations to serve the meal. Her bright blue eyes twinkled. She loved cooking for the family. She reminded me of Mrs. Claus with her wire-rimmed glasses, white coiffed hair, and gentle spirit. Gram knew I loved to eat the bread dough, so she always saved me some. I ate it as fast as I could, savoring the gooey dough, but it always made my little belly bloat. I'd pull up my dress or shirt and say, "Gram! Look at my big belly!" She would just laugh.

After lunch on those Sundays, the whole family would play games. Sometimes, even Dad played. One of my favorites was red rover, but croquet was also fun. If the weather was bad, we would play cards inside. Only the women and we three girls played cards. We have played pitch or pinochle since we were little girls. The only time I ever saw Gram mad was when she would lose at cards. She was super competitive. Mom would tease her and laugh while Gram stomped her foot.

Gram was so pure and innocent. One time when the two of us were out shopping, she was pulled over by a policeman for speeding. (Gram had a heavy foot on the pedal.) Somehow, she talked her way out of a ticket and gave the officer a $50 bill for letting her go. After the officer left, she turned to me and said, "We mustn't tell Grandpa about this since he doesn't know that I keep a hidden fifty in my pocket book for emergencies like this." I said, "Gram, I won't say anything. Your secret is safe with me!" We returned to their home later that day. When Grandpa came home that night, the first thing Gram said to him was, "Pop, I was pulled over for speeding today, but I gave the officer a $50 bill that I keep hidden in my pocketbook and he let me go free." Grandpa just shrugged like he didn't really care. I couldn't believe it! She turned to me and whispered, "I just can't keep any secrets from Pop, I would never forgive myself." Pure and innocent, like I said.

Grandpa and I had a special bond as well. When I was little, I used to sit on his lap and sing (to the tune of B.J. Thomas's "Raindrops Keep Falling on My Head"): "Raindrops keep falling on my pawpaw, but that's not worrying him! No, raindrops keep falling on his head, they keep falling. It's just me and my pawpaw!" He called me his "Pooh Bear," after Winnie the Pooh. He used to have all of these dry sayings, like, "If you hang around with shit, you're gonna get some on you." He used to tell me to choose my friends wisely. I can still hear him talking about me to others, "That Pooh, she's as strong as horseradish! There ain't nothing she can't try to do." Like I said, we had a special bond, just as he did with Stormy and Steph, each in their own unique way.

Outside in their front yard was a huge oak tree that shaded the little country home and was surrounded by hills and levees that provided a gentle breeze. Grandpa had fashioned a big swing on the old

Stormy, Steph, and me at our grandparents' farmhouse, on the hammock, 1973

oak tree, and my sisters and I used to push one another on it. They also had a brown, yellow, and orange striped hammock that we used to lay on together. At night, we looked for shooting stars among the millions of twinkles in the sky, and during the day we would look for shapes in the clouds. On both sides of their driveway, Gram had planted lilac bushes, and in the summers, the outside and inside of their home smelled so sweet from the blossoms. To this day, every time I smell lilacs, I think of those treasured times.

Gram and Grandpa lived on about five hundred acres and raised cattle and pigs. They had two farrowing houses for the pigs on the east side of their home and in between was a little creek where my sisters and I used to play. One summer day, after we got bored with the creek, we walked up to the farrowing house. We were looking at all of the pigs when I suggested that we crawl in what looked like a wide tunnel. Stormy said something like, "I don't think that's a good idea." I decided to prove her wrong and jumped—only it wasn't concrete like I thought! It was pig sewer, all the way up to my neck! I crawled my way out and ran to the house, made my way through my grandparent's back porch, and started stripping my clothes off by their laundry room, which was just off of the kitchen. I stunk so bad!

My mom, gram, great-grandma, and aunt were in the kitchen washing and drying the dishes from lunch and chatting with each other. I vividly remember Great-Grandma Coose asking, "Did someone fart? What is that smell?"

They turned around and saw me taking the last of my clothes off.

"What the hell did you do?" Mom shouted.

Stormy and Steph had made it into the house by then and told them that I had jumped into the sewer. They laughed so hard! I was humiliated. It took three baths to get the stench off of me and out of my hair.

Stormy and I worked on the farm during the summer and after

school. Our jobs were to clean out the farrowing houses, trim the fence rows with hand clippers, sometimes mow the lawn (when I was older after the electrocution incident), and help out with the livestock. I enjoyed riding the horses to get the cattle up from one pasture to another. I felt like such a cowgirl! It was fun. We also helped out with castrating the pigs, which was not one of my favorites by any means. I literally learned what squealing like a pig meant. We had dogs—purebred collies who were more like our siblings. Penny Pincher was the mom, and her son Sugarbread was more than happy to play with us all day. We would play tag with them for hours, running around the house until they "tagged" us with their noses and laughing so hard my stomach hurt.

We all played softball, so we were at the diamond nearly every weeknight. Mom was coach for each of our teams. Just like her mothering, she was a passionate coach. My first team was called the Pixies. I played shortstop and was one of the fastest runners.

I lived to play, but learned early that it wasn't good if my dad came to our games. When we got home, he would berate us and tell us we played like sissies. My older sister got the brunt of the verbal abuse, as she did in all other areas of our lives. I think Mom became conditioned to never try to stop his assaults since she would then get it even worse. Dad had even knocked out all of Mom's teeth during one violent fight. Mom said he hit her so hard that the force of the blow spun her into a backflip.

* * *

Beauty is life when life unveils her holy face.
But you are life and you are the veil.
Beauty is eternity gazing at itself in a mirror.
But you are eternity and you are the mirror.

—**KAHLIL GIBRAN**, *The Prophet*

When I was young and too naïve to understand why the dark times had to come, I didn't realize what fueled the fire. I was too little to understand alcoholism and how it can alter one's personality. One evening while we were having dinner, my dad was in one of his "moods." Everyone just sat, quietly eating. Suddenly, he picked up the kitchen table and threw it on Mom, screaming, "Why is everyone so damned quiet?"

I sat in my chair, looking at Mom as she cried and tried to get the heavy table off of her hips where it had landed. We knew better than to cry because if we did he would be in our face telling us to grow up. As usual, nothing further was said about the incident, only that he was sorry the next morning and that he would try to be better.

We were supposed to act happy then, like it never happened. I can still see the black and purple bruises on Mom's hips, which lasted for weeks after it happened. To this day, it makes my stomach turn when I think about how I had to sit on his lap as he said he was sorry but Mom had made him mad, and he would not do it again. I knew better—there was always a next time.

The fights were too horrific to witness, so Stormy would take Steph and me into her room where we would wait it out and pray that Mom would be okay. We begged her time and time again to leave him, but it played out over and over: we would pack our bags, get into the car, and say, "Let's go!" Then, Dad would come out to the car and ask Mom if he could talk to her. She would go inside and tell us to wait in the car. Sometime later, she would come out and say that everything was okay and tell us to come back inside and unpack.

I remember having a terrible sinking feeling as I walked back into that house. I just wanted her to be strong enough to get away from him; I was too young to understand the weight of responsibility that was on her shoulders. You see, Mom got pregnant when she was just

16. Dad was 21. She had to quit school and have Stormy when she was 17. I suppose Mom and Stormy received the most abuse since they were the first ones he turned to in his raging, drunken fits. I would eventually get mine.

Try to be at peace with everyone, and try to live a holy life, because no one will see the Lord without it.

—HEBREWS 12:14

CHAPTER 8

I will send an angel ahead of you to
protect you as you travel and to bring you
to the place which I have prepared.

—**Exodus 23:20**

One winter day I was out helping Dad with the farm. I must have been about 12. I was driving the old orange Chevy truck. Dad would open the gates, allowing me to drive through, then I'd wait for him to close the gate and get back in the truck. We had done this many times.

Almost always the dogs followed us, and today was no different. As I was about to pull through the first gate, Dad yelled, "Gun it!" When I began to slowly drive through to be wary of the dogs, he yelled even louder, "Dammit, I said gun it!" Afraid of what he would do if I didn't, I punched on the gas and got through the gate. He yelled, "Stop! Now, get out of the truck!" I put it in park and got out. He said, "Now, come over here and see what you've done."

I walked to where he was standing to see my dog on the ground, broken and bleeding. I started crying as I looked up at my father. His cold blue eyes stared right at me, and he started laughing.

I ran as fast as I could, away from there and away from him. I didn't care about the repercussions I might suffer later; I hated him at that moment. My dog was dead. I ran into the house and screamed for Mom. When I told her what happened, she cried with me and said she was sorry, but sometimes people could be very cruel. I don't know what else she could have said. There were no words for a situation like that.

* * *

Happy is the person who remains faithful under trials, because when he succeeds in passing such a test, he will receive as his reward the life which God has promised to those who love him.

—JAMES 1:12

I idolized Stormy; she was everything I wanted to be. Stormy was beautiful, like Raquel Welch, with a perfect body, gorgeous hair, exquisite face, but mostly, the most gentle and pure heart of anyone I knew. Stormy was kind to everyone, no matter who you were, and always stood up for anyone who was being bullied. I suppose you could say she was just like Mom. In high school, Stormy was voted most popular, most athletic, and friendliest. She was amazing. Some of the best days of my childhood were spent with Stormy. We understood what was going on and bonded; she was my best friend. My sweet little sister Steph was too young and, in my mind, had escaped most of the ugliness, and for that I was grateful.

Stormy was three years older than me. When she was sixteen, she began dating. On Friday and Saturday nights, I would watch her get ready. She would put on her makeup, dry her hair, put in the hot rollers, and get dressed up. All the while, we would talk about where she and her date were going, what they would do, etc. I'm sure I got on her nerves, but she never said anything. When her date picked her up, I would go to her room and watch as they drove down our driveway and then the long gravel road that led out to the blacktop that went to town or the highway. I watched until I had to squint to see the car fade away. I would sit on her bed and sigh, wishing I could go with them.

Stormy, 1982

Your pain is the breaking of the shell that encloses your understanding.

Even as the stone of the fruit must break, that its heart may stand in the sun, so must you know pain.

And could you keep your heart in wonder at the daily miracles of your life, your pain would not seem less wondrous than your joy;

And you would accept the seasons of your heart, even as you have always accepted the seasons that pass over your fields.

And you would watch with serenity through the winters of your grief.

—KAHLIL GIBRAN, *The Prophet*

On Sunday evenings, if Stormy were allowed to go out, she would ask me if I wanted to go. I was like, "Are you freaking kidding me?! Yay!" Once we were away from the house, Stormy and her boyfriend Sam would let me drive the Jeep while they made out in the back seat. We told Mom and Dad that we were going 4-wheeling. I would drive down muddy gravel roads and through ditches, learn to do donuts, and, in the winter, blast through snowbanks. We would smoke cigarettes and drink beer. We had the best time. I was just grateful to be with her and out of that house.

As time went on and we got a little older, the abusive episodes and raging fits at home grew in frequency and force. There was something brewing in our house. I could feel it inside me like strong winds and dark clouds in a summer storm, and we were in the midst of it. The only place I felt peace was at Gram and Grandpa's house. In their home I found refuge, as I am sure my sisters did as well. It was the only place where I felt safe and protected.

My sisters and I took turns spending Friday nights at their house. Often, when we were younger, I remember fighting over whose turn it was since we all wanted to go. It was Gram's home where we would go when the fighting got too bad or if we had to get away. More times than I can remember, we had to call them in the middle of the night to please come pick us up. They were always there for us and usually didn't ask too many questions.

We had three working farms and employed three farmhands to help run them. Two of them, Jack and Jesse, were pretty young—I would guess in their early to mid-twenties. They were twins and very handsome and charismatic. I secretly had a crush on Jesse, but never breathed a word to anyone!

It was shortly after they came to work for us that I began to notice a difference in our house. Mom seemed to be getting stronger, emotionally anyway. All of the farmhands had lunch with us every day at our kitchen table. Mom always had fresh lunch meat with lettuce and cut up tomatoes from our garden. It was delicious. Since Jack and Jesse began joining us, there was a lighter feel at the table and more joking and laughing. Even Dad seemed better. I wouldn't know it until much later, but Mom was falling for Jack. Looking back now, I think it gave her the strength to finally say, "I've had enough."

On the night that everything in our house changed, Stormy must have been about 16. She had gone out on a date with Sam, so it must have been a weekend night. I think her curfew was 12:30. I awoke around 1:00 a.m. from the yelling and screaming. Stormy was a little late, and Dad had been drinking. He locked her out of the house and wouldn't let her in. Mom pleaded with him to open the door. I don't remember much past this, only that my next memory is of us with Mom in the car driving to Gram and Grandpa's home. It must have been 2:00 a.m. or later, but they were up and welcomed us in. I was so grateful to be in their home. Gram made us something to eat as we told her what happened. She just shook her head. After eating, we were exhausted and went to the bedrooms to get some much needed, peaceful sleep.

The next morning, Dad came over to their home. This was unusual. He never acted up around Gram and Grandpa, so they never saw that "side" of him. He came in and acted so gentleman-like, it made me sick. He apologized, again, and said it wouldn't happen again. I was in the back blue bedroom listening and wanted to scream, "Yes, it will!" But I had to remain silent, as usual. Eventually, we ended up going back to that house. I hated it.

It didn't last. I'm not sure how much longer we stayed there, but it wasn't very long. We ended up moving in with Gram and Grandpa. Their home was three bedrooms, one bath, so it was a little tight, but who cared? We were out of that house.

As the new school year started, I told myself it would be a better year for all of us. We stayed with Gram and Grandpa through the fall, but Mom eventually found a house to rent. We were so happy together. I felt free and good for the first time I could remember; but this too wouldn't last long.

Jack began coming over to the house to see Mom, but they had to be careful and discreet. It was our secret. I was so glad to see Mom happy and in love. She was glowing. Stormy and Sam were still dating and seemed equally as happy. We would all play cards together; joking and laughter was bountiful in those days.

Mom and Dad's divorce was proceeding. In the settlement, they had to sell almost everything. If I remember correctly, the only thing not auctioned off was the house and the land where we had lived. I was at the auction and remember seeing my dad look so sad that I felt sorry for him. My eyes got wet with tears because I had never seen him like that. He was not only losing his family, but everything else he had worked for. It was sad, for all of us.

Somehow, Mom got granted the house and the land that it was built on, so the four of us moved back in. I felt weird, moving back in that house, into my bedroom and the other rooms where so many bad memories had been made. The feelings eased with some time, as we made new, happier memories there. But this wouldn't last long either.

I don't remember when Dad found out about Mom and Jack, but he did. All hell broke loose. It was around this time that Stormy found out she was pregnant; she was seventeen. Dark times loomed once again for us. I cried so hard the night she told me. She had asked me if I wanted a ride home from softball. As we sat in the car outside of our house, she said, "I have something to tell you." I was hoping it would be something good. She said, "Freddie, I'm pregnant."

She had called me Freddie since I was young. It went back to when I was little and she used to tease me that my real name was

Winnifred. I would cry and argue that it wasn't, eventually getting Mom involved to tell me that she was just joking. Winnifred got shortened to Freddie, then just Fred over time. Even my friends and eventual boyfriends called me Fred.

Now here she was using that silly name to tell me this big news. She cried with me and we hugged while I realized my sister would never be the same.

Through all this, Dad began harassing us at home. He would break into the house while we were out and do who knows what. He had taken up with a ruthless man from town who was known to be a terror. I remember answering a phone call in which Dad was on the other end with this guy telling me they were going to come over, kidnap me, and kill me. I vividly recall the language they used: "You pussies aren't going to live to see another day when we are done with you." Then, they would laugh hysterically. I would hang up the phone, shaking so violently with fear. I didn't know what to do. Mom had extra locks installed on the doors, which was about all we could do, I suppose.

While Stormy and Sam took time to discuss what their plans were, she stayed with us at the house. Sometimes Sam stayed, too, and that made me feel more secure. Having a man in the house I hoped would protect us if something happened. Jack stayed over, too—not all the time, but occasionally. I liked it when both of them were there.

One night, Mom and Jack had gone out to grab a drink, Stormy and Sam were somewhere, and Steph was sleeping over at a friend's house. I was home alone and scared. I made sure all of the doors were locked, all the outside lights were on, and the dogs were in front of the house. I knew they would bark if someone were coming.

Sure enough, Dad knocked on the door later that night asking to come in. I told him no. He broke in and grabbed me, threw me in his truck, and took off. I was so scared that I must have blacked out. The next thing I remember is being at the bar where Mom was with Jack and my aunt Chub. He told me to stay locked in the truck or I would be killed.

I watched in horror as he yelled at my mom outside of the bar. It looked like he was going to hit her, so Aunt Chub got in between them. My dad put his big hands around my aunt's neck and lifted her high off of the ground. I saw the wetness saturate her jeans as she peed her pants—she must have been so scared! He put her down after some men came to the rescue, telling him to stop it. They took him away and were trying to talk to him as Aunt Chub came to the truck where I was. Outside the window she asked me to unlock the door. I said, "No, he will kill me!" She said she would not let that happen. We left and went to Gram and Grandpa's house for the night.

For a time after this, I think things quieted down some. It must have because I can't recall anything else significant happening. I have no one to call to ask since Stormy, Mom, and Steph are all gone. It makes it difficult to tell this story since I believe I used blacking out as a defense mechanism to survive. It is times like this that I realize how many losses I have had to endure. I miss them all so much.

The Lord is my protector; he
   is my strong fortress.

My God is my protection, and
   with him I am safe.

He protects me like a shield; he
   defends me and keeps me safe.

He is my savior; he protects me
   and saves me from violence.

I call to the Lord, and he saves
   me from my enemies.

Praise the Lord!

—2 SAMUEL 22:2–4

CHAPTER 9

Let us be brave, then, and approach God's throne, where there is grace. There we will receive mercy and find grace to help us just when we need it.

—**Hebrews 4:16**

I suppose Mom eventually began to run out of money from the sale of the assets. She got a job as a fitness instructor/salesperson at an all-ladies fitness center on the outskirts of St. Louis. Jack broke up with her about the same time, and I witnessed her devastation. She was so depleted that she got very, very sick, but she managed to work while trying to get better.

Mom worked with several other ladies who would become her best friends and our second moms. They were so good to us girls. I looked up to them as I did my mom. I was so grateful for their support of Mom during that difficult time. After being there only a few years, Mom worked her way to becoming the number one salesperson. She was always a natural with people since she was just herself, and most people loved that about her.

Mom, Steph, and I moved to a rented apartment in the city. I was in middle school and Steph in elementary, so we had to switch schools. I suppose the kids in elementary school were not too bad, but the kids at my school were, for the most part, horrible. When I would step onto the bus in the mornings, they would say very loudly, "Who let the pig on the bus?" The whole bus laughed at me. Then, to top it off, no one would let me sit in a seat. For months, I rode to school standing up the entire way. At lunch, I sat quietly by myself.

Inside, I began to lose hope in anything. We had little to no money; we couldn't even buy sugar to put in our tea or Kool-Aid. We lived on plain spaghetti noodles with occasional tomato sauce. God bless Mom. She was working night and day trying to provide for us, but it was difficult. Dad didn't pay any child support, so it was up to Mom to pay for everything. My only solace was going to Gram and Grandpa's and seeing Stormy on occasional weekends.

Stormy and Sam got married on December 10, 1982. Steph and I were bridesmaids, and Gram, being an incredible seamstress, made Stormy's wedding gown and our dresses. It was quaint and beautiful,

Five generations: Mom, Great-Grandma Coose,
Gram, Courtney, and Stormy, 1984

an evening ceremony with just family in attendance. Courtney was born the following February, and I instantly fell in love with the little girl.

Stormy and her new family were living in the house we grew up in since it was free and they were trying to get by on the little salary Sam made. Things were tough for them, too. I went to see them as often as I could to spend time with Courtney. I was so miserable when I went back to the apartment, as well as at that horrible school. I had an idea. Maybe I could live with Stormy and Sam and help take care of the baby. I was afraid to leave Mom and Steph, though. As time went on, I became more and more depressed. Feelings of desperation were developing inside me, and I couldn't fight it.

Somehow, I made it through that school year and went to live with Stormy and Sam for the summer. I was as happy as possible being with my sister and my niece. I helped Stormy as much as I could, constantly looking for things that needed to be done to "pull my weight" and not be a bother to them since I was so grateful to be there. The summer flew by. Soon, I found myself going back to that stupid school. I dreaded it, but hoped maybe that year it would be different, maybe even better. It wasn't; the only thing that changed was that I met a friend, Sally, who would have lunch with me. The bus ride was the same awful experience.

By the end of the first semester, I couldn't take it anymore. I told my mom that I needed to live with Gram and Grandpa and go back to my hometown school. She said okay. I remember her dropping me off and trying to hold back her sobs as she left to go back to the apartment.

But it didn't turn out as I hoped. At my old school, things had changed. Kids treated me like I was an outsider instead of someone they all knew and had been friends with. They looked at me differently somehow. Or was it just me? My old best friend Christy was still my friend but had become best buds with someone else. On top of it, everyone knew of the nasty divorce and everything else that had happened. I felt that I didn't belong anywhere anymore.

I was so depressed that I went deep into myself and didn't talk to anyone. I felt so alone. I wanted to die. I planned my suicide carefully. I didn't want to hurt anyone and I felt extremely bad about what I was planning to do, but looking back, I was in a place so dark and depressed that I couldn't see the light of day.

Some of the kids were going to a concert and somehow, I ended up going. We drank a lot that night, which was not planned but probably gave me the courage to make my attempt. When I got back to Gram and Grandpa's, I took an entire bottle of pain pills and passed out, but not before asking God to forgive me. It was St. Patrick's Day, March 17, 1984. I was 15 years old.

* * *

Do not start worrying: "Where will my food come from? or my drink? or my clothes?" (These are the things pagans are always concerned about.) Your Father in heaven knows that you need all of these things. Instead, be concerned above everything else with the Kingdom of God and with what he requires of you, and he will provide you with all these other things. So do not worry about tomorrow; it will have enough worries of its own. There is no need to add to the troubles each day brings.

—MATTHEW 6:31–34

I woke up the next day, not believing that I was alive. I was groggy, shaking uncontrollably, and very weak. I stumbled to the bathroom and started to take a shower. Then, I began dry-heaving in the toilet. I was in a very bad shape.

I called Mom and asked her to please come. When she got there, she asked me what was wrong with me. I told her what I had done, and we drove to the emergency room. The doctor examined me, took blood, and ran other tests.

It's difficult to remember, but I recall waking up in a hospital bed with my ears ringing so loudly that I could barely stand it; my stomach and heart hurt as well. I looked over to see Stormy holding Courtney by the bedside. She was crying, and said, "Freddie, why?"

I started to cry and said I didn't know, but I did—I really wanted to die. I couldn't take any more of this life. But, I didn't say it. The doctor was talking to Mom; I overheard him say that if I had taken the whole bottle then I should not be alive. They didn't believe me. Dad came storming in, saying, "Do you know how stupid you are?" I started shaking and crying. The doctor asked him to leave, telling him he was not helping the situation. I was grateful for that.

I told Mom and Stormy how sorry I was and that I didn't mean to hurt anyone. That was the truth! I don't know how it was decided, but I was taken to a psychiatric hospital in St. Louis. It was evening when Mom drove me, and I had no idea where we were going. We went into the hospital room, which was in a basement. I thought that was weird, but went in anyway. I was given a gown and asked to lay on the bed. The nurses proceeded to chain my wrists and ankles to the bed. I couldn't move and began screaming and screaming. Mom started to cry and ran out of the room. I was in such a terrible state of mind that they had to sedate me. I don't remember anything for days.

The hospital is a vague memory for me. I only remember talking to a psychiatrist one on one and being in therapy groups with other kids. They made us listen to grasshoppers at night. In the morning we had to do 20 jumping jacks and push-ups. I hated it, but there was nothing I could do about it. *I put myself in here,* I told myself time and time again. *I deserve this.*

I recall a few of the other kids who were in there with me. One young woman, Tricia, had a shopping problem. I thought that was so weird. She used to steal her parent's credit cards and go on shopping sprees until the credit cards were maxed out. As we got deeper into therapy and Tricia and I got closer, it turned out that her father was sexually abusing her. Her mom didn't know about it. Apparently, she was using this "escape" as her way of dealing with it. I am not sure what happened to her and her family.

Slowly, I began to open up to the therapists, too. We talked about everything: Dad, the divorce, the way the kids treated me at school, and about me and how I didn't feel that I fit in anywhere in this world. I learned that it's not all about fitting into a certain group, but about being comfortable with yourself and your decisions. Eventually, I felt myself getting a little stronger. I began to realize that I was reacting to the situations surrounding me. I could choose to deal with whatever was happening in a different way and not take everything so personally. I felt such remorse for putting my mom and family through what I had done. I had to accept that, though; it was done and over. The past is what it is.

After one month in the hospital, I was released. It was the end of April and my sixteenth birthday had just passed. I was eager to get my driver's license and move forward with my life, finally.

School was a little better, as far as the kids went. I was embarrassed about my suicide attempt because everyone knew about it, but thought, "What can I do?" I was still here in this life and was trying to be "happy"—whatever that was. I got my license the first part of May.

On the last day of school, May 25, 1984, I was driving my sister Steph and two of our friends home from school so they didn't have to ride the bus. After I dropped off the friends, Steph began to cry as I drove, softly at first, then more hysterically. I asked her what was wrong. She said she didn't know. Looking back, I think she sensed something bad was coming.

I kept driving toward my grandparents' house on the two-lane blacktop road leading into town. We came upon an accident with a few drivers pulled over. It looked like the accident just happened; a car had flipped and landed on its hood.

Weirdly, my home economics teacher was there and approached my window. She asked me if we were going straight home, and I said yes. She said, "Go straight there!" When I asked why, she said, "Please, just go." She looked so sad.

I drove for about a mile and then stopped at a little convenience store just off the road, the only one in town. I ran in and asked the owner if she knew what had happened. She said, "You don't know? It's Stormy." I screamed, "No!" and ran back to my car, turned around, and hurried back to the accident. I had not recognized her car since it was so messed up.

When we got there, I jumped out and tried to run to her; she was lying on the grass with a pink blanket covering her body up to her neck. Someone grabbed me before I could reach her—I didn't know who—but he held me back and said, "You don't want to see your sister right now." I said, "Yes, I do, let me go!" He would not. I noticed that her head was moving from side to side, so I could tell she was alive. I fell to my knees and cried, praying to God to please let her be okay.

Steph and I were following the ambulance down the interstate when, somehow, I saw Mom on the other side of the highway. I flashed her my lights, and she turned around to follow us. Thank

God I saw her! Once we got to the hospital, I told Mom that it was Stormy.

We were not allowed to see her for what seemed like an eternity. Then, the doctor came out and said they had to transport her to a bigger hospital in St. Louis, as they did not have the means to treat her injuries. Once again, we followed the ambulance to the hospital in the city, about 45 minutes away. We sat in the waiting room, holding each other and praying that she would be okay.

But then the doctor came out with the devastating news. He told us there was nothing more they could do for her but that we could go see her. Sobbing, we walked into her room.

I heard the beeping of the machines. I noticed she only had one shoe on. She looked like she was sleeping, but there were cuts on her face and head. I could not believe this was happening. As we approached her bedside, the machines flat-lined.

She was gone! No! Oh, my God, no!

I kissed her face and tried to hold her, but the nurse pulled me away. Mom, Steph, and I were crying hysterically, trying to hold onto each other.

Before the funeral, Mom suggested to Steph and me that we write Stormy a letter to place in her casket. She said to write anything we wanted to say to her but didn't have a chance.

I wrote my sweet sister a letter and told her how sorry I was and that I loved her so much and that I would miss her every day of my life. She had always been my best friend, my inspiration for living. I told her that I would watch over her precious daughter for her. I didn't understand how God could take her away, not only from us, but from her daughter who needed her. *Why?* I kept asking. *Why?* Courtney was only 15 months old.

For the funeral, we had to borrow clothes from my aunt, since we didn't have anything appropriate to wear. She brought us suits with matching hats, since it was raining so hard. The only things I remember about that day is that God must have been crying in heaven because of all the rain and Dad commenting to me how ridiculous we looked. Maybe we did, but who cared? My sweet sister, my best friend was gone; who cared what clothes we had on? Nothing mattered anymore.

To be honest, I don't remember very much for the next several years, only bits and fragments and that Mom, Steph, and I went to counseling. We would go once a week. Sometimes we went in together, while other times we went in separately.

At one session, the psychologist's assistant Jeanine joined us. As the others talked, I remember silently talking to Stormy in my head. Jeanine looked at me and said, "Wait! What were you just thinking about?" I told her I had been talking to Stormy. She said, "I just saw a bright light, right above your head. It was Stormy!" Apparently, Jeanine was a bit psychic and could see or sense spirits.

The psychologist told us to support each other, to keep communicating with each other, and I specifically remember him telling us to paint our toenails together. He prescribed Valium for us so we could sleep at night.

For a long time, I was very angry at God and I thought that he didn't exist anymore. I hated him. I couldn't even listen to music because every song made me think of Stormy. I had lost all of my faith.

Hail, Mary, full of grace, the
    Lord is with thee.
Blessed art thou among women, and
    blessed is the fruit of thy womb, Jesus.

Holy Mary, Mother of God, pray
    for us sinners, now and at the
    hour of our death. Amen.

—**AVE MARIA,** *a Catholic prayer*

CHAPTER 10

i carry your heart with me(i carry it in
my heart)i am never without it(anywhere
i go you go,my dear;and whatever is done
by only me is your doing,my darling)
                                    i fear
no fate(for you are my fate,my sweet)i want
no world(for beautiful you are my world,my true)
and it's you are whatever a moon has always meant
and whatever a sun will always sing is you

here is the deepest secret nobody knows
(here is the root of the root and the bud of the bud
and the sky of the sky of a tree called life;which
grows higher than soul can hope or mind can hide)
and this is the wonder that's keeping the stars apart

i carry your heart(i carry it in my heart)

—E.E. CUMMINGS

Mom began seeing Dave shortly after Stormy's death, but I can't remember exactly when. I remember being very protective of Mom, though, and I regret that I wasn't very nice to Dave for the first few years. I didn't want to see her get hurt anymore. They got married on December 28, 1985. Eventually, I would grow to love him dearly and consider him as my dad. Dave was always there for Steph and me with whatever we needed. He was, and is, a wonderful father.

Looking back now, the rest of my high school years seemed to fly by. That was probably a good thing, since I didn't really fit in with "the crowd" and felt alienated. I knew I was far from normal with all that we had been through. I looked at life differently than most kids my age. I suppose we were humble but, at the same time, more appreciative of what we had. I just didn't understand why my life had been so difficult so far. Perhaps it wasn't meant to be understood; instead, like Mom said, "Keep your faith and hold onto what we have left."

Steph and I were very close with Mom and Dave, and of course, Gram and Grandpa. I played volleyball and worked part-time at a fast-food restaurant. In the summer, Mom, Dave, Steph, and I would play slow-pitch coed softball. I dated around but never really got serious with anyone until I met Billy's dad.

We were young, way too young to get married. When we got married in the summer of 1987, we were only nineteen. I don't want to talk about our brief marriage. I will only say that I will be eternally grateful for our relationship producing Billy. I will always love that family.

I was 20 years old when Billy was born. I cried the first time I saw him, thinking he was the most beautiful baby I had ever seen. An overwhelming love for him burst inside of me. I wanted to wrap myself around him with love and protect him from everything.

My sole purpose in life was to be his mom, and I was so grateful to have him.

Although we didn't plan it that way, it turned out that Mom was also pregnant at the same time I was. Once we got over that surprise, we loved sharing that special time. I was due in November 1988 while Mom was due in February 1989. As I grew out of my maternity clothes, I would send them to Mom so she could grow into them. As usual, we talked daily and kept each other updated on our progress and how we were feeling. Maybe it was the prenatal vitamins, but I felt great until the final month, when I was so ready to give birth. I was so tired and felt "heavy." Besides, I was so ready to meet this new soul!

That's how Billy was born three months prior to my brother Lucas. Later, when that first marriage ended (we were just too young), Billy and I lived with Mom and Dave for quite some time. The two boys grew up as though they were brothers and stayed that close.

I vividly remember them when they were around six or seven, eating their breakfast cereal at the kitchen bar. If one of them burped or farted, the other one would puke, literally. (They had very weak stomachs.) Needless to say, mornings were interesting. Mom loved them dearly, but used to say, "They could fuck up a wet dream." They were always breaking something in the house, messing up Dave's basement workout room, or falling out of their treehouse.

Billy called my mom Nina, and Mom adored Billy as if he were her own son instead of her grandson. Billy remained close to all of us throughout his brief life, even when he went to live with his dad after Beau's dad and I married. Sometimes he would tell me things that a mom doesn't always want to hear, but I was always grateful for his trust in me. One time when he came to visit from one of his jobs in Louisiana, he showed me his tongue piercing. I said, "Billy, why did you do that? Didn't it hurt?" His reply was, "Nah, it didn't hurt.

The ladies love it, especially when I put in the vibrating stud!" My mouth must have dropped to the floor because he threw his head back laughing.

    I have many regrets as a mother to him, but there is nothing I can do about it now. I try to let these regrets go. It is very difficult, and sometimes I think they stay buried deep inside of me. I remember the last time we were together. He was taking me to the airport on Christmas Eve in 2008. I had flown in for Grandpa's funeral. As we drove the 45 minutes or so to the airport, I told him how very proud I was of him, and that I was sorry for anything I ever did to hurt him. He had said, "Mommy, I am the person I am today because of you. I love you." I hugged him so tight at the airport and told him I loved him so much. As he drove away in his new black Silverado, I had a strange feeling that something was going to happen. I prayed to God to keep him safe and that I would see him again. I told myself that surely, after all that our family had been through, that no more could happen. I was so wrong.

Let us keep our eyes fixed on Jesus, on whom our faith depends from beginning to end. He did not give up because of the cross! On the contrary, because of the joy that was waiting for him, he thought nothing of the disgrace of dying on the cross, and he is now seated at the right side of God's throne.

—HEBREWS 12:2

CHAPTER 11

The most obvious lesson in Christ's teaching is that there is no happiness in having and getting anything, but only in giving.

—**Henry Drummond,**
The Greatest Thing in the World

The years went by quickly, and eventually I met Beau's dad and got married. I was 30 years old when Beau was born. I didn't know I had so much love in me until the day he was born, when I realized I loved him as much as Billy and felt the same connection to this little soul. It was almost like I "knew" him.

My boys, how I loved them! I thought of my dad and how he had treated me and my sisters, and for the first time, I felt sorry for him. I felt compelled to write him a letter. I wrote that I sincerely forgave him for all that he had done to me, that the only thing that remained in me was my love for him. I had forgiven him and needed him to know it, even if he didn't respond (which he didn't). It didn't matter to me. I had let it go—and had let it go with pure love in my heart.

I had read many books on life, death, spirituality, and love since I was a young girl. Something occurred to me when I thought about my dad. Maybe he loved me so much that he had agreed to come into this life to "toughen me up" for all of the things I was going to have to endure. After all, didn't I believe we choose our parents as well as our family?

Two of my favorite books, *The Book of Love* and *The Expected One* by Kathleen McGowan, helped shape my beliefs, along with many, many other books that I read. The ideas resonated with me, and I began to memorize the passages that were most meaningful. Somehow, I felt the truth in the writings about families of spirit, which meant to me that our "spirit family" is not necessarily our "blood family."

Mom used to tell us that just because a man fathers a child, that doesn't make him a dad. Also, I believe that we are here for a purpose, and that each of us plays an important part in aiding one another in our destinies. I believe in the search for God. I had been in such a dark place that I tried to take my own life, but by the grace of God,

I made it through and began my search for him and his purpose. If I hadn't, I would have remained in a world of darkness.

That is what I believe to be true. I knew it was my destiny to have both of my boys in this life and felt a connection to them that extends beyond the present lifetime. We are forever tied to each other. When I mailed the letter to my father, I felt light, free, and surrounded by love. It was a wonderful feeling. Now, I could enjoy my life with the boys!

But the Spirit produces love, joy, peace, patience, kindness, goodness, faithfulness, humility, and self-control. There is no law against such things as these.

—GALATIANS 5:22–23

CHAPTER 12

May the Lord himself, who is our source
of peace, give you peace at all times and in
every way. The Lord be with you all.

—**2 Thessalonians 3:16**

Tuesday, December 28, 2010

I had done a lot of thinking as I sat beside my mom for those days in the hospital. Finally, on her anniversary with Dave, she got to go home. I did not leave her side—I couldn't. She was in a good mood when we got her home. She was talking normally, said she felt good, and was cracking jokes. She kept saying that she now knew Stormy and Billy were fine and that she was no longer worried about them. She was almost glowing.

I went back home January 2 and went back to work. On January 13, 2011, I went in for an ultrasound for the suspicious area on my breastbone, followed by a biopsy on February 4. The doctor called the following Monday and asked that I come in to discuss the results. On February 8, Rod and I found out that I had breast cancer.

I just stared at the doctor and the nurse, who was holding a pink folder. Unbelievable. My first thought was that maybe I would see Billy sooner than I thought. But, since we didn't know the extent of it, I didn't think too much of it. I was primarily still concerned about Mom. Her treatments started that week. They needed me there since Dave was working and Steph had her four young girls at home. My brother Lucas was still in college hours away. So, the next week I flew back to St. Louis to take care of Mom, putting my cancer far from my mind. I had to be there for her. On March 2, I resigned from my job.

I began to save all of Mom's voice messages to me so I could hear her sweet voice when the time came. How I wish I had done that for my beloved son! I was trying to process all of this: Billy's passing, Mom's cancer, my cancer. It was so overwhelming. Mom and I had discussed before how much sadness our family has had to endure over the years. We talked about how God must have a plan in all of this. She reminded me to hold onto the good, stay strong, and never lose faith.

The first week of April, Rod and I went to Moffitt Cancer Center in Tampa for another MRI for me. I just wanted it over. I knew Mom was worried about me and my cancer, but I was not. My only concern was for her. Steph called me to tell me that Mom was very tired all of the time and should not be driving anymore, but Mom was too stubborn to listen. How I wished I were there. Not just to help, but for us to be together while we could.

I didn't want to believe it was happening. What was I going to do without my mom? She had always been my best friend, my rock, my inspiration. I told myself that God had a plan, and that was why this was happening—that was why Stormy and Billy weren't there. I had to have faith that he knew the plans he had for all of us. I realized that Mom would be with them before I would and wanted to ask her to tell them how much I loved and missed them—but I couldn't.

On April 13, my birthday, all I wanted was for Mom to be okay, for some miraculous healing to take place. I prayed for this daily. I tried to stay busy while we waited for my surgery later in the month. I took Billy's things from his funeral and accident out of my dresser and placed them in a wicker basket with a lid. I couldn't look at any of the papers—the police report, death certificate, etc. But I felt it was time to move them into storage. I couldn't move his suitcase out from under my bed—not yet. I still liked to smell his clothes. They smelled like him—woodsy and fresh. On the days when the yearning to see him was too much, I would wrap his olive-colored hoodie from Abercrombie around me and breathe in his smell, savoring the essence of him.

My surgery was on April 25. The surgeon said she thought they got everything out and recommended radiation treatment. Thankfully, there would be no chemotherapy. However, in two days, the doctor called to let me know they didn't get all of the cancer out and I would need a second surgery.

I didn't want to tell Mom or Beau because it was just more bad news and they would worry, but Mom heard it in my voice. Mom called me back that day and told me she and Dave were going to drive to be with me for my surgery. I was happy but very worried about how she could handle the 20-hour drive. I prayed to God to give her strength. Rod and I were in shock and Beau was very worried, but I told him that I was going to be okay. He asked why all of this bad stuff was happening to us. I told him that God had a plan and we had to have faith. Above all, we had to keep praying!

My second surgery was on May 2. Mom went with Rod and me to Tampa and spent the night before my surgery in a nearby hotel. The surgeon said she was confident that all of the cancer cells were removed, but she had to scrape my breastbone to get it all. She put me on pain medicine and ordered rest. I was sore and groggy from the medicine but very grateful Mom was there. We all went home later that day. Mom and Dave left on May 4. I wondered if I would see her again and prayed to God that I would. Rod took good care of me while I recovered and I knew, as I had for some time, that I couldn't have endured all of this without him. I said a prayer of thanks to God for Rod and my family.

One week after my second surgery, Rod, Beau, and I flew to Houston along with Rod's parents to attend his son Brad's college graduation. It was a nice celebration. From Houston, we flew to St. Louis for my brother Lucas' college graduation. We drove 2.5 hours to his school with Mom and Dave. I worried about Mom making the trip because she was very weak. At the auditorium on the campus, there are so many stairs to the entrance. But I was amazed at Mom's determination. Slowly, we made it up the stairs. We found seats on the auditorium floor for Mom and Dave, and the rest of us climbed up to mid-level to watch. I couldn't take my eyes off of Mom, though. She amazed me.

Immediately after the ceremony, we drove back to our little hometown for a benefit that Dave's company had planned for Mom. It was called "Trivia Night." Little did we know that almost 600 people would be waiting for us. I was in awe of the community support—all for Mom. She had so many friends and people who loved her. That night, over $17,000 was raised to help pay for Mom's treatments. Mom gave a funny, heartwarming speech that was genuine, pure, and truly Mom.

> Hi, friends! This generosity and compassion you have shown is unequaled. God has blessed us with so many awesome friends! Thank you so much for all your many prayers, cards, food, and offers to drive me to the hospital, and all of our local churches have had Wendy and me on their prayer lists for some time now. We have even had masses said for us over in, where is it? Rome, yeah, that's it! [The crowd roared with laughter.] I told David that's pretty good for a Presbyterian! I feel good about that! I mean, God loves us all!
>
> I love all of you very, very much. Please remember to take time for your faith, family, and your friends. God bless each and every one of you, and please remember to be kind to one another. It would mean a lot to me.

Mom got a standing ovation for her speech and so much laughter erupted when she wasn't sure if it was Rome or not. Mom amazed me, as always.

For life, with all it yields of joy and woe
And hope and fear, ...
Is just our chance o' the prize of learning love,
How love might be, hath been indeed, and is.
—ROBERT BROWNING,
"A Death in the Desert"

CHAPTER 13

Rod, I am deeply grateful that God chose you to be my beloved husband. Our Creator, God above, unites us in love, and it is only through love that heaven is created on Earth. As above, so below. I pray that we may live each day together, knowing there is no separation between God and us.

So now, in the presence of God and these our family and friends, I take you to be my wedded husband, promising with Divine assistance to be a loving and faithful wife, so long as we both shall live.

—My vows to Rod at our wedding

I began radiation treatments in June. On my initial visit to the radiologist, I drove myself to the office, scared with the anticipation of what was going to take place. I was marked up with black Xs on areas near my breasts that were to be targeted by the machine. These would stay on my body for the duration of the treatments. I would go every day, five days a week, for six weeks. From the onset, it was a degrading experience. I had never had so many people look at my breasts.

The second week into my treatments, on June 25, 2011, Rod and I got married. It was a beautiful ceremony with just family and a few friends on the beach. Steph flew down to stand with me and called Mom so she could hear the ceremony. It was magical. Rod has truly been my angel through all of this. I say again, I can't imagine getting through all of this without him. I am grateful every day for him!

Rod and me at our wedding on the beach, 2011

After two weeks of radiation, I told the doctor I had to take a break and fly up to take care of my mom. He reluctantly said okay, even though I was going with or without his consent. I was completely exhausted, but my mom and my family needed me.

I stayed a little over two weeks. I took Mom to her treatments every day, leaving at 7:00 a.m. and not getting back to her house until afternoon. We drove my grandparents' car, a silver Grand Marquis. We used to joke as we were pulling out of the gravel drive, saying, "The Silver Bullet rides again!" Then, we would both laugh.

Mom was so tired that most afternoons, after we got her settled, she slept. I took care of the laundry, cleaned the house, and cooked for the family. Steph came over in the afternoons with her four daughters to help out. It was nice having all of us together.

Even going through this, Mom still cracked jokes and laughed. She watched the Food Network and the Game Show Network, switching between the two almost every day, all day. One day as I was sitting on the sofa with her, the hosts on a show were cooking up Maine lobsters with a special lemon butter sauce. As they finished the plate, Mom looked over at me and said, "Well, that's fucked up that we can't have one, too!" We laughed and I said, "I know, right?" When she tried to run the vacuum, I asked her to please let me do it. Mom would say, "I'm just doing a little lick and a prayer run."

The doctor had told her that the treatments would probably cause constipation. She got very constipated and tried over-the-counter laxatives, but they didn't work. So, she decided to try prunes. Mom asked if I thought two or three prunes would work. I didn't have any idea. She told me she would try taking two.

I can still see her shuffling out of the bathroom with her little head covered by a white-laced knit cap to cover her bare head saying, "Well, two's not enough!" I asked her if anything at all came out and her reply was, "Nits and gnats!"

At night, we sat out on their front porch, sipped some wine, and watched Steph's four girls play in the yard. I went to pick up Gram from her place at the assisted living facility on Sundays so she could spend the day with us. I thought of her strength: how she had lost a son, a daughter, her husband, her granddaughter and grandson, and now would soon be losing Mom. She had never, since I had known her, lost her faith in God and her ability to stay positive in her outlook on life. She told me that you can't question God's will, only stay faithful to his plan.

She was such a pure, gentle spirit and was always my sweet Gram. I adored her. We talked on the phone every Sunday, no matter what. At the end of our conversations, she would say, "I love you, a bushel and a peck and a hug around the neck!" I would repeat it back to her. It was our ritual.

Courtney and Gram with Courtney's dog Callie on a Sunday visit at Mom's, 2011

Mom, me, and Steph on Mom's front porch, watching the kids play, 2011

I went back on July 17 to resume my radiation treatments. I was so exhausted. I felt like a robot, driving to and from the radiation facility. Like Mom did when she was taking her treatments, while I was in the machine and the loud, clicking noises began, I prayed.

I said the Lord's Prayer, sang "Praise God, Father, Son, and Holy Ghost," and said prayers for Mom to please get better. In all, I finished six weeks of radiation. My last treatment was on August 15, so I flew back to St. Louis the next day to take care of Mom.

While I was there, she asked me for a favor—if I would please compile and download all of her favorite songs. We made a list, and it turned out to be about 4½ hours. She said she wanted this playlist to be played at her service when she passed. I told her of course I would do this for her, but inside I was crying, *No!* How was I going to do this? It was so very hard.

I only stayed for five days as something was wrong with me. I was bleeding uncontrollably. I went to the gynecologist at home the following Monday, and he informed me that I needed a total hysterectomy. My breast cancer was fed by estrogen progesterone, or, as they called it, ER/PR positive. Besides, I had had cancerous cells before on my cervix. The best solution was to remove everything. Great. Beau had just started the new school year that day too. They had scheduled my surgery for later in August, but it was rescheduled for some reason that I can't recall. Just as well—I was tired and needed to rest.

While Beau was at school, I logged onto iTunes and began downloading all of Mom's songs. It didn't take as long as I had expected. As they downloaded, they would play and I would sit at the desk and think: *Mom!* I couldn't believe it was happening. It was so hard, but I told myself I had been through worse—at least I thought so.

I thought of how important it was to cherish every moment we have with those we love. We can never get those moments back.

How easy it is to miss those moments when our schedules and lives get so busy that we get caught up in getting this or that project done. I thought of some of my friends who luckily have never lost any of their loved ones. Do they know how fortunate they are? When was the last time I really looked into my loved ones' eyes and told them I loved them? When was the last time that I was really present, in the present? Why does it have to be that we realize how much we love someone after it is too late, after they are gone? I know Gram said we cannot question why things happen; nonetheless, I did have questions. I had to believe there was a reason, that God's plan was playing out the way he designed.

As I waited for Mom's playlist to finish, I began searching the internet. I'm not sure what I was looking for—just some inspiration to give me strength or hope. I came across some song lyrics that reminded me of God's love for all of us here, and I sent up a prayer of thanks to Jesus. I felt his presence around me more than ever. The song is "If You Want Me" by Ginny Owens.

I don't know how I found it (or maybe it found me!), but, wow, did it hit home. I felt like it was written especially for me to read at that moment. It made me remember that we are never alone and that God is always present in our lives through the best and most horrific times. I will not give up; I will walk through the valley if he wants me to, with faith that his love and grace will go with me.

The most important [commandment] is this: "Listen, Israel! The Lord our God is the only Lord. Love the Lord your God with all your heart, with all your soul, with all your mind, and with all your strength." The second most important commandment is this: "Love your neighbor as you love yourself." There is no other commandment more important than these two.

—MARK 12:29–31

CHAPTER 14

Happy are those who know they are spiritually poor; the Kingdom of heaven belongs to them! Happy are those who mourn; God will comfort them! Happy are those who are humble; they will receive what God has promised!

—**Matthew 5:3–5**

In September 2011, Rod and I finally got to go on our honeymoon after a three-month delay because of my treatments. He took me to Lake Louise and all over Alberta, Canada. It was the most magical vacation I had ever had.

On our first day, we drove from Calgary to a little town called Canmore where we walked and had lunch. The air was cool, crisp, and smelled like Christmas, the perfect place for our first stop. We ate burgers and had a beer at the Grizzly Paw, then walked across the street to a little soap shop to buy some bath salts, homemade in town. It was such a cute and quaint little mountain town; I fell in love with it.

We then drove to our rented cabin on Storm Mountain near Banff. The cabin was rustic and homey, with a log-burning fireplace as the only heat. We unpacked and relaxed, and Rod started a fire. The main lodge was next door so once we were refreshed, we walked to the restaurant and had a glass of wine by the huge fireplace before sitting down for dinner. Rod loved his organic chicken with angel hair pasta and I had a trio of salads. It was just a great day!

Our cabin was nice and toasty by then, and we fell asleep to the crackling fire. The next morning, we woke up at 3:00 a.m. probably because of the time change. We waited for a few hours until the lodge opened to get coffee. Rod went and brought two cups for us, and we sat on the front porch of our cabin and watched the most spectacular sunrise: beautiful shades of reds, pinks, and orange. It was breathtaking.

At Kootenay National Park, we embarked on a 5-hour climb up Stanley Glacier Mountain. It was incredible and unbelievable that we did it. I knew Rod could do it but had serious doubts about myself. The smell of the air was so pure, so fresh and clean. The streams and waterfalls were breathtaking; I had never seen anything so beautiful. I took in the views, thinking how I wished Billy, Beau, and all of our family members could experience this. When we reached the top of the mountain we felt so great. I kept thinking: *Seven weeks after all that radiation and I climbed 5,000 feet and feel this good.* I thought of my grandpa, who always told me, "Take deep breaths, Wendy."

Starving now, we drove into Banff and ate bison burgers with blue cheese and a few beers. After, we drove to Lake Louise and viewed the gorgeous glacier-fed lake that had the most beautiful blue water I have ever seen. We walked around the lake and strolled through the Fairmont Hotel.

I guess the blue-cheese burgers didn't set well with my stomach because I had such awful gas pains. I was trying to hold the gas in, but as we were walking by a group of young men, I let one slip out. It was "hot," and I knew it would stink something terrible. Rod turned to me and said, "Wow, one of those boys let out a stinker." I chuckled to myself, but didn't tell him it was me.

We went into the hotel to look around the shops when another one slipped out, only this time we were the only ones inside the shop. Rod looked at me and said, "It was you!" We laughed so hard we were crying. This was the first time I had passed gas in front of him and was totally embarrassed. To this day, we still laugh about that. I think the laugh was much needed, even if it was at my embarrassment.

We drove back to our cabin. I took a long, hot bath in the old-fashioned claw-foot tub with the bath salts we had bought in Canmore. It was luxurious. We watched a movie on my iPad since we had no television and fell asleep with the fire once again in the background.

We woke up a little later the next day, around 6:30, and the lodge had coffee ready—bonus! We got ready and drove to Bow Lake. They say it's one of the most beautiful drives in North America, and I agree. We stopped for breakfast at Bridges before heading back to Banff to tour the Fairmont there. The hotel was magnificent and looked like a castle nestled in the mountains. We purchased some things to take home, along with souvenirs for Beau. The next morning, we got up early and left for Jasper. We took the Glacier Parkway, another popular North American drive that was incredibly beautiful.

We stopped at Peyto Lake, then went to Athabasca and hiked up to the actual glacier. As we walked up, snow began to fall in huge flakes and the temperature dropped to zero. It was snowing so hard that I could barely see anything. I had missed the snow since moving to Florida.

Me with the glacier behind me, 2011

Rod at the top of the glacier, 2011

The Lord's unfailing love and
    mercy still continue,
Fresh as the morning, as sure as the sunrise.
The Lord is all I have, and so
    in him I put my hope.

—LAMENTATIONS 3:22–24

CHAPTER 15

You were born together, and together
   you shall be forevermore. ...

Love one another, but make not a bond of love:

Let it rather be a moving sea between
   the shores of your souls.

Fill each other's cup but drink
   not from one cup. ...

Sing and dance together and be joyous,
   but let each one of you be alone,

Even as the strings of a lute are alone though
   they quiver with the same music.

> Give your hearts, but not into
>> each other's keeping.
>
> For only the hand of Life can contain your hearts.
>
> And stand together yet not too near together:
>
> For the pillars of the temple stand apart,
>
> And the oak tree and the cypress grow
>> not in each other's shadow.
>
> —**Kahlil Gibran**, *The Prophet*

We returned the first week in October. I was so grateful we had had that time together. It was truly magical and allowed me to forget about everything else going on back at home for a while.

My surgery was the following week, on October 12, Mom's birthday. I was told I had to rest for six weeks and to expect the symptoms of menopause to begin rather quickly since I was "tiny." At least that's what the doctor said. Holy hot crap! The hot flashes started within two weeks. I was totally unprepared for them. I would try to describe them, but that could be another book in itself. I felt like an old lady, with all of my female body parts either removed or operated on. Poor Rod, he had to start sleeping in his sweatshirts because I had the air condition going full blast, plus two fans blowing on the bed at night. Even then, I was freaking hot.

After five weeks, I flew back up to take care of Mom. She was getting weaker and weaker, but her spirits were high. She was an inspiration. I drove her to her last treatment and was there to witness the "ringing of the bell." I had witnessed countless other patients who beamed as they rang the bell, signaling their final treatment. As Mom did, they were all so proud and glowed from their courageous fight.

I hoped most of them beat whatever battle they were fighting. Mom hugged everyone as she left, even though she didn't know them.

Mom and I spent that visit talking about a lot of things—how we should build our riches in heaven, not on earth, and about a sign she would give to us to let us know she was okay. She decided on a butterfly. It didn't have to be a specific one, just any kind of butterfly would be Mom's message to let us know she was with us and that she was okay. I still couldn't believe this is happening.

She also asked me one other thing: to please continue to cook for the family whenever possible. Family time, gathering in the kitchen for one of our famous home-cooked meals, was one of the most important times. I know, I learned from the best—Mom and Gram. Mom's lasagna was the last meal we made together. To this day, every time I make it, I can feel her beside me, as if she's saying, "Thanks, honey!"

Each member of the family was dealing with Mom's situation in our own way. Sadly, Steph started drinking heavily, and early in the morning. When I asked her why and to please stop, she didn't talk to me for two weeks. God bless Mom's husband Dave, who was always so optimistic. He just kept saying, "She's going to be okay, it's all going to be okay." Gram just went with it, cherishing every moment that she still had with her daughter. Lucas was home and working, and pretty much kept things inside. Like with Billy's death, he just couldn't talk about it. Rod and Beau were in Florida, with school and work.

Even Mom's beloved yellow Labrador Ozzie was trying to deal with it. One day when we returned from one of her treatments, Ozzie took one of Mom's house slippers out to the front yard, dropped it, and peed on it. Then, he looked back at us as if to say, "I'm pissed off, too!"

Mom used to say: "If you lock your husband and your dog in the trunk of the car, who do you think is going to be happy to see you

Mom and Ozzie, her beloved Lab, 2010

when you open it up?" Of course, she was joking, but Dave always knew he was second to Ozzie.

How did I deal with it? I cried, prayed, cried some more, sipped white wine at night, and prayed some more. It was in God's hands, as is everything, even if we don't realize it.

I went back home to Florida right before Thanksgiving. I wanted to have a nice holiday with Beau and Rod and the rest of his family who were there. Plus, I had follow-up visits with my gynecologist and oncologist, who was still checking me every six months. I hated it. After my cancer, radiation treatments, and hysterectomy, I became anxious whenever I went in for a checkup. The nurses would have to take my blood pressure a couple of times since it would be too high—they called it "white coat syndrome." After I took several deep breaths, it would come down to a more reasonable level that the nurse felt comfortable recording in my chart.

Mom had decided that for Christmas that year, the whole family should go up to the Wisconsin Dells for a family ski trip. This would be her last present to all of us. Our gang flew up to St. Louis, then everyone drove up to the Dells together.

Mom had rented a huge house for all of us. There was Mom, Dave, Ozzie (of course), Lucas, Steph, Chris, and their four girls, Courtney, Austin, Rod, Beau, and me. All of us except for Mom, Dave, and Rod went skiing. Mom stayed in bed most of the time, but would come to the resort later in the day to watch the kids ski and then we would have dinner. We played games like Catch Phrase at night and laughed until we cried. Beau said he had never seen Rod laugh so hard. It was a wonderful, bittersweet five days together. We got home January 2, 2012.

The month of January flew by. I tried to stay busy at home with cooking for Rod and Beau, keeping the house clean, and gardening. I went back to Mom's in the first part of February. The three-year anniversary of Billy's passing was coming up, so Mom and I visited his grave and left flowers and crystal angel figurines by his headstone. We held onto each other and wept. I didn't know it then, but it would be the last time Mom visited his grave. The next time she would visit him would be in heaven. We were both exhausted, mentally, emotionally, and physically. The end was coming.

Families of Spirit draw their strength from one another in times of need. Let your strength now be given unto you from us, your spirit family, for it is our responsibility now to provide this. This is how heaven on Earth is created; through the strength of enduring love. And remember, God is in and all around you!

—**My last note to my mom after she was diagnosed with brain cancer**

CHAPTER 16

No one lights a lamp and then hides it or puts it under a bowl; instead, he puts it on the lampstand, so that people may see the light as they come in. Your eyes are like a lamp for the body. When your eyes are sound, your whole body is full of light; but when your eyes are no good, your whole body will be in darkness. Make certain, then, that the light in you is not darkness. If your whole body is full of light, with no part of it in darkness, it will be bright all over, as when a lamp shines on you with its brightness.

—Luke 11:33–36

On March 15, I flew back to help with Mom. She was progressively getting worse and had a stroke. The doctor said he could run all kinds of tests on her, but it wouldn't change the situation. He asked her what she had been doing, and Mom slurred, "Well, I can tell you I wasn't having sex!" The doctor's mouth dropped open. She still had that dry sense of humor.

He asked us all what we wanted to do since she was in her final weeks, if not days. Dave and Lucas sat still, not knowing what to say. I was numb, but I looked at the doctor and said, "Mom just wants to go home." He said, "Okay, let's get hospice set up to come to the house."

I had been there all day so I asked Dave if I could go on ahead of them and start dinner. I had to get out of there. I couldn't breathe. I cried most of the way back to Mom's house.

We got Mom settled in at home that night. After I cleaned up the dinner dishes, I went to Steph's for the night. I was completely exhausted. Steph and I sat outside on her deck, sipping some wine. We didn't talk much—neither of us knew what to say. Our days with our sweet mother were numbered, and there was nothing we could do about it.

On Tuesday, March 20, I arrived at Mom's early so Dave could go to work. The hospital bed, oxygen tanks, and all kinds of equipment were delivered by the hospice team. It was so shocking and overwhelming to see it all.

Mom was slipping fast. I tried to do all I could to make her comfortable. I wanted to make her better, but I couldn't. Mom was too weak to walk, so I had to just about carry her to go to the bathroom or when she wanted to go outside to smoke. (The doctor said she could smoke as much as she wanted at this point.)

Steph got there later in the morning so I was able to take a shower, dry my hair, and put fresh clothes on. When I came out into the living room where Mom was lying on her hospital bed, I took her hand and sat down. I asked her if I could get her anything.

Mom looked at me and gasped. She said, "Oh my, you are so beautiful!"

I said, "No, I'm not."

"Oh yes, you are—you have no idea what I see!"

It was like she was seeing a new person. I felt like she was seeing my aura or my soul or something. I started to tear up and massaged her hand as she closed her eyes.

Steph and I were at her side all day, taking turns for breaks and cooking for the family's dinner that night. Steph took her girls home, and I told her I would be there later. I stayed until about 8:30, then told Dave I would be back at 6 a.m. the next day.

I got to Steph's and was mentally and physically exhausted. I felt like my body was on autopilot. That night, the tears wouldn't be contained, and we both cried until our eyes were red and swollen.

We were trying our best to take care of all Mom's needs. When her nose got clogged, I tried to get her to blow her nose, but she didn't have the strength. I used a baby nose aspirator. She didn't like that and quietly said to me, "That'll do, donkey!" (It is a line from the movie *Shrek*.) Still making jokes! Steph and I had to laugh at that one.

I didn't know what else to do. Mostly, I prayed.

The days were a fog and went by so slowly. Steph and I told Mom how much we loved her and what a wonderful mother she had been, and we thanked her for all that she had done for us. I told her I was sorry for anything I had done that may have hurt her, the tears a continuous stream down my face. I thought of my beloved Billy—how I didn't have a conscious chance to tell him all of the things I would have told him if I had known he was going to pass from this world.

I knew what was coming, yet I was so not prepared for it. Yes,

I had told Mom all that I wanted to tell her and I knew that she knew how much I loved her. Nonetheless, saying goodbye is one of the hardest things in life, especially the last goodbye—until we are together again.

The only joy greater than union...is reunion.

—**KATHLEEN MCGOWAN,** *The Book of Love*

CHAPTER 17

You would know the secret of death.

But how shall you find it unless you
    seek it in the heart of life? ...

If you would indeed behold the spirit of death,
    open your heart wide unto the body of life.

For life and death are one, even as
    the river and the sea are one.

In the depth of your hopes and desires lies
    your silent knowledge of the beyond;

And like seeds dreaming beneath the
    snow your heart dreams of spring.

Trust the dreams, for in them is
    hidden the gate to eternity. ...

> For what is it to die but to stand naked in
> the wind and to melt in the sun?
>
> And what is it to cease breathing, but to free the
> breath from its restless tides, that it may rise
> and expand and seek God unencumbered?
>
> Only when you drink from the river of
> the silence shall you indeed sing.
>
> And when you have reached the mountain
> top, then you shall begin to climb.
>
> And when the earth shall claim your
> limbs, then shall you truly dance.
>
> —**Kahlil Gibran**, *The Prophet*

Week of March 31, 2012

Looking back, it was such a surreal, amazing time. I hated to leave Mom's side. I wanted to be with her as much as I could. I prayed to God and Jesus that she wasn't in any pain. I prayed that his will be done, in all things. I was past trying to ask for a miraculous healing—I didn't have that hope anymore. As I sat by her side, I kept holding her hand and telling her how much I loved her and how she had always been my best friend. My precious mom. How many times can a person's heart break?

One afternoon, Mom began lifting her arm, motioning her hand like she was taking things from below and putting them in a cabinet or something above it. This went on for quite some time. When the hospice nurse got there, I asked her if she had seen anything like it.

She said Mom was communicating with spirit and that she had seen this often. Mom was preparing for her departure. I had that feeling that this was what she was doing.

After the nurse left, I was alone with Mom. I watched her, amazed by what she was doing. She would lift her hand high, take something in her hand, bring it to her lips, kiss it, and then put it back. Time after time, for over an hour. In a way, it was a beautiful thing, because she looked so happy and at peace.

As I sat by her side, she suddenly began to take in big gasps of air, the kind you do when you see someone that you haven't seen in a long time. Then, she raised both hands like she was going to embrace someone. Mom was not speaking anymore, but I asked her, "Who do you see? Is it Billy and Stormy?" Tears were rolling out of the corners of her closed eyes, and then she nodded ever so slightly.

I couldn't help the flood of tears myself. I was witnessing a reunion of the most sacred type. I asked her to please tell them both how much I loved and missed them. I said, "Mom, if you see Jesus, you can go with him to the light. Tell my son how much I love him and take care of him until I get there!" She nodded, tears still escaping from the corners of her closed eyes.

A part of me was so happy for her, to be reunited with Stormy, Billy, Grandpa, and so many others, and of course, Jesus. She had waited for so long. It was such a bittersweet blessing to watch this reunion. I will never forget it. My faith in God and Jesus was renewed to a new, higher level than ever before in my life. I vowed to cherish it, every day.

I believe this was Mom's last gift to me while she was still on this earth: to allow me to witness her reunion with her beloved family and to show me what I have to look forward to, when God calls me home. I know I will be with them again. We will embrace each other, laugh, cry, tell each other, "Good job," dance to the music of heaven, and finally, stand in awe of God's greatness and understand how he wove such a perfect plan for each of us. My soul quivers with anticipation for that moment to come.

We had her music on again on that day. When "Carry On My Wayward Son" by Kansas came on, with the lyrics, "Lay your weary head to rest, don't you cry no more," I sang it to her.

No more tears for Mom, she had cried enough. I said an inward prayer, "Thank you, Jesus, God, angels, for everything, for our family, for Mom!"

The Lord your God is with you;
>   his power gives you victory.
> The Lord will take delight in you, and
>   in his love he will give you new life.
>
> —**ZEPHANIAH 3:17**

CHAPTER 18

Jesus said…, "I am the resurrection and
the life. Whoever believes in me will live,
even though he dies; and whoever lives
and believes in me will never die."

—John 11:25–26

On the evening of March 31, Mom began struggling to breathe. I asked Steph if she told Mom goodbye yet, and she said that yes, she had; I asked Lucas, and he said yes. But when I asked Dave, he said no. I told him that I thought she was waiting for him to tell her goodbye. We left the room so he could talk to her.

After a few minutes, he came outside to where we were all waiting on their front porch and said he had told her. We went back in, and she had passed. I couldn't believe it. She was laying there, so at peace. I knew she was already in heaven—somehow, I just felt it. God bless you, Mom.

Mom had strict instructions for after she passed. These instructions were in all of our envelopes that she had prepared for us. On a single sheet of paper, she wrote these exact notes to us:

> Do good to all people in accordance to God's will. Be kind to one another. Build your riches in heaven, not on earth. Please be gentle on yourself—we all make mistakes and have regrets. All of life is a lesson, and we learn from our mistakes. Give yourself time. Praise God from whom all blessings flow. Trust in the Lord! God will give you strength. My beloved Grandpa Coose lay in the hospital. He looked at me with his beautiful eyes and said, "It's going to be a long night, Lindy." I knew he would be gone by morning. I had never lost a member of my family at that time—I think I was around 19. I came home that night, opened my Bible to give me direction to a scripture that would give me comfort. It said to go to Psalm 27. It has given me comfort every time I read it. It was read at Billy's funeral. I don't read the Bible like I should, but I cherish that chapter. I miss my grandparents. They were such wonderful people. Someday we will all be together again and what a reunion that will be!

She asked that we read "Desiderata" often and included a copy of the poem in our envelopes.

Go placidly amid the noise and the haste, and remember what peace there may be in silence. As far as possible, without surrender, be on good terms with all persons.

Speak your truth quietly and clearly; and listen to others, even to the dull and the ignorant; they too have their story.

Avoid loud and aggressive persons; they are vexatious to the spirit. If you compare yourself with others, you may become vain or bitter, for always there will be greater and lesser persons than yourself.

Enjoy your achievements as well as your plans. Keep interested in your own career, however humble; it is a real possession in the changing fortunes of time.

Exercise caution in your business affairs,
for the world is full of trickery. But let
this not blind you to what virtue there
is; many persons strive for high ideals,
and everywhere life is full of heroism.

Be yourself. Especially, do not feign
affection. Neither be cynical
about love; for in the face of all
aridity and disenchantment it
is as perennial as the grass.

Take kindly the counsel of the
years, gracefully surrendering
the things of youth.

Nurture strength of spirit to shield you in
sudden misfortune. But do not distress
yourself with dark imaginings. Many
fears are born of fatigue and loneliness.

Beyond a wholesome discipline, be gentle with yourself. You are a child of the universe no less than the trees and the stars; you have a right to be here.

And whether or not it is clear to you, no doubt the universe is unfolding as it should. Therefore be at peace with God, whatever you conceive Him to be. And whatever your labors and aspirations, in the noisy confusion of life, keep peace in your soul. With all its sham, drudgery and broken dreams, it is still a beautiful world. Be cheerful. Strive to be happy.

—**MAX EHRMANN**, "Desiderata"

* * *

Mom wanted to be cremated and didn't want a big public service, but she was loved by so many people that would've been impossible. Steph and I drove to the funeral home to meet Dave to go over the plan for the service, which would be April 7. Something in me clicked with the dates: Billy's accident was on February 7 and his funeral on February 13. Mom passed on March 31 or 13 backwards, and her funeral was on April 7. Is there something to this? I have to believe that there is and that it is a validation of God's plan—that it is connected somehow. I feel the truth in this.

For Mom's service, we set up photos of her and played the music that she wanted in the background. As I sat and waited for the service to begin, I listened to the music and remembered making the playlist for her. It seemed like so long ago, but really was only a few months prior to this day. How did I do that? By the grace of God, I told myself.

In our little hometown where I grew up, hundreds of people lined up around the block, waiting to get into the little chapel to pay their respects. Dave got up and said a nice speech in honor of Mom. I had brought a poem that Stormy had written when she was little and planned on reading it, but was unable to. I suppose I didn't have the strength or the courage; I'm not sure.

Here is the poem:

Flowers for Mother
By Stormy

I never have a special day to give flowers to my mother.
I give them to her every day to show how much I love her.
When I sweep the kitchen floor or care for baby sister,
Run errands or make the beds, I am giving flowers to
   my mother.

She's always sewing buttons on or mending things to wear,
When I come home from school I always find her there.
Are you surprised that I find her dearer than any other?
I'm sure by now you know her name.
Of course, she is my mother.

We decided, as Mom wished, that we would only receive people from 4:00–6:00 p.m. At the end of the service, we played her two favorite songs, at her request: "It's a Fine, Fine Day," by Tony Carey, and "Roll Me Away," by Bob Seeger. Mom used to sing these songs all the time. She used to talk about what a reunion there would be, in heaven, when she passed. I can still see her dancing and singing to "Roll Me Away." She loved music.

After Mom's music finished, we walked across the street to the only little bar in town and made a toast to her. It's what she wanted. I felt bad that we didn't have time to accommodate all of her friends, but we invited them to come with us if they could. We did the best that we could and felt that she was proud of us .

My sheep listen to my voice; I know them, and they follow me. I give them eternal life, and they shall never die.

—JOHN 10:27–28

CHAPTER 19

This would I have you remember
 in remembering me:

That which seems most feeble and bewildered
 in you is the strongest and most determined.

Is it not your breath that has erected and
 hardened the structure of your bones?

And is it not a dream which none of you
 remember having dreamt, that builded
 your city and fashioned all there is in it?

Could you but see the tides of that breath
 you would cease to see all else,

And if you could hear the whispering of the
 dream you would hear no other sound.

But you do not see, nor do you hear, and it is well.

The veil that clouds your eyes shall be
> lifted by the hands that wove it,

And the clay that fills your ears shall be
> pierced by those fingers that kneaded it.

And you shall see

And you shall hear.

Yet you shall not deplore having known
> blindness, nor regret having been deaf.

For in that day you shall know the
> hidden purposes in all things,

And you shall bless darkness as
> you would bless light.

—**Kahlil Gibran**, *The Prophet*

We came back home that Sunday, April 8, after the memorial. It felt like I had been gone for so long. We resumed our schedule, with Rod working and Beau's school, golf, and baseball.

Two weeks later, on the morning of April 21, I woke with severe pain, to the point I was dry-heaving. Rod drove me to the ER where we discovered I had a 9mm kidney stone that was stuck in my urethra. I have never had so much physical pain. I was given strong pain medicines and had a stent inserted into my body to drain my kidney. I would have surgery the following Friday.

Looking back, I realize how depleted I was, both physically and mentally. I thank God for Rod, my angel and my steady companion through all of the things we have been through. I am so thankful for his support and light in my life. He once told me after we first began to get serious in our relationship that Billy had sent him to me, and I truly believe it. Thank you, too, Billy!

Once I recovered from my surgery and felt strong enough, I needed to decide if I wanted to go back to work or not. I am not the type to just sit around—I have to stay busy. I've been this way my whole life, maybe so I wouldn't have time to think. For me, thinking too much is not good. I interviewed for an onsite real estate sales position. I heard they were considering three people so I just decided to let the universe direct me with God's plan for me.

Meantime, Rod, Beau, and I left for a badly needed vacation to Jackson Hole, Wyoming. It was a long travel day but we sat in first-class—a first for me and Beau! They served us quesadillas for lunch and cheese enchiladas for dinner. Boy, did we have gas! The ride down over the mountains was very, very turbulent—one of the worst we had ever experienced. It certainly didn't help the gas we all had and were trying to hold in while on the airplane. We all started tooting as soon as we landed and continued to baggage claim. People would slowly try to step away from us as we waited for our luggage. We couldn't stop laughing. We really polluted that place. It felt so good to laugh again!

I woke up early the next morning, around five o'clock. We were going whitewater rafting that day. This was the first time for me and Beau, and we were super excited. We left at seven to meet up at Sands, just outside of Jackson Hole. The first leg of the float was very scenic and quiet, almost like a gentle float trip—very beautiful. We stopped at a camp alongside the river where the guides prepared breakfast for us. I was sitting on log enjoying the sun and scenery when a huge yellow and black butterfly fluttered around my head. My eyes got wet with tears, and I said a silent thank you to Mom. She was with me.

Butterfly from Mom, 2012

After eating, we switched to a smaller boat. Beau and I volunteered to sit up front, which was supposed to be the most exhilarating place to ride. It was awesome! We got completely drenched several times, especially by a 6-foot wave that crashed over the boat. Beau said it was the best experience he had ever had. That made my heart smile.

We spent the next day in Jackson, first picking out our pictures from the rafting trip then visiting the Wildlife Art Museum. Later, we drove to Jackson Lake Lodge to check in for our 4-day stay there. It's a very large campus-like atmosphere, and our room had a nice front porch. But I wasn't feeling good and already knew I had pneumonia, which was confirmed at a local clinic. I couldn't do anything except lay in bed for two whole days until finally the antibiotic kicked in and I felt a little better.

We were finally able to go on the 3-hour horseback trail ride. I was grateful for the time with Rod and Beau and that I was feeling better. We explored Old Faithful and the geysers at Yellowstone, visited the mud volcanoes, and took hundreds of pictures. At night, the three of us played games and laughed and laughed. We made sweet memories that will last a lifetime.

On our last day, I received a phone call from the broker I had interviewed with offering me the onsite job. I gladly accepted and said I would start the following week.

The summer flew by. I stayed busy with work and taking care of things at home. I missed Mom terribly, but tried to keep my mind off of that.

Most days I was okay, but other days it hit me like a wave. In November, around Billy's birthday, I was having a difficult time. I was driving home from work on November 13, the day after his birthday. I couldn't control the tears. When I stopped at the red light to turn into our subdivision, I looked up in the sky and could not believe what I saw: God had written "B I L L Y" in the sky. It was sloppy but nonetheless, to me it was there. Wow. I told him how much I loved and missed him. Then, one of my favorite songs that has always reminded me so much of him, even before he passed, came on the radio, as if a second validation from him.

Thanks, Billy! I love you!

Love gives naught but itself and
 takes naught but from itself.
Love possesses not nor would
 it be possessed;
For love is sufficient unto love.

—**KAHLIL GIBRAN**, *The Prophet*

CHAPTER 20

Peace is what I leave with you; it is my own peace that I give you. I do not give it as the world does. Do not be worried and upset; do not be afraid.

—**John 14:27**

Rod, Beau, and I stayed busy with work and school. In between, we had some awesome travel adventures.

Rod took us to Italy in the summer of 2013. It was the trip of a lifetime! We arrived in Rome and rented a car. Rod couldn't find the clutch in the car because there was no clutch even though it was a stick shift, so we had to ask the rental agent to show him how to drive the car. While Rod was setting the rearview windows into position, we watched an old guy who didn't know how to drive European cars either. He accidentally pressed on the gas, then popped the hood of the car as it accelerated forward, nearly hitting his wife. Thankfully, he stopped in time. We all laughed hysterically.

We headed towards Positano, stopping in Naples and Pompeii to tour the ruins and eating at a little pizza café before getting on the highway. Rod went to use the men's room and discovered the toilets didn't have seats. He came out looking flushed, so we asked him if he was okay. He informed us that he felt like he was doing leg squats and his legs were shaking while he was relieving himself. Beau and I laughed so hard we were crying.

Me and Beau in Positano, Italy, 2013

In Positano the next morning, Rod and I got up early and went down to a local coffee shop. We ordered two Americanos and both got the shakes since they were so strong. Beau had croissants with Nutella in our room. On the way to a walk on the beach, Beau's stomach started making loud rumbling noises. He said he ate too much Nutella. He rushed into the restaurant from the night before, since we knew where the bathroom was. We couldn't stop laughing when he came out. We walked down the hundreds of stairs down to the beach.

Driving to Ravello and the Amalfi Coast, the roads were so narrow and winding that I made myself look straight ahead to keep from getting carsick. We visited a church in Ravello where the smell of summer honeysuckle was so sweet, I thought it must have been what heaven smelled like.

The next day we finally slept in until 7:30 a.m. The hotel staff brought us breakfast: Americano cappuccino coffee, hot chocolate, and fresh baked croissants with Nutella. (We asked Beau to please go easy on the Nutella.) We took a ferry to the Isle of Capri, where we toured the Blue Grotto. We had to lie down to enter the cave's

Rod, Beau and me touring the Blue Grotto, 2013

Me, Rod and Beau in Rome, 2013

opening, which was just big enough for the little boat to enter. Once inside, the sunlight came through the opening, illuminating the cave with an indigo light that seemed to shine up from below the water. Some of the boat guides began singing in Italian, while some of the other tourists jumped into the water even though it was icy cold. I was in awe; it was so beautiful.

We left for Florence the next morning, where we toured the Duomo, St. Maria Cathedral, and Uffizi. At my request, we took a day-trip to see the Volto Santo (Holy Face) in the Cathedral of Lucca.

I was awestruck when I came to the Holy Face. I had read about this sacred sculpture in the *Book of Love*, where Kathleen McGowan describes how one of Jesus' disciples, Nicodemus, carved a near-perfect likeness from the walnut wood of his Lord, Jesus Christ. The carving is said to be holy and that miraculous healings have taken place there. I got goosebumps standing in front of the glass-enclosed holy relic—I had that déjà vu feeling that I had been there before. It was the highlight of the trip for me. Even now, I long to return there.

We traveled throughout Italy for the rest of the amazing trip. We visited all of the cathedrals, museums, and ruins during the days and at night would have wonderful dinners followed by gelatos for Rod and Beau. Back in our hotel rooms, we would play cards nearly every night before going to bed. We were exhausted when we returned home, but we all agreed it was the best trip we had ever been on.

In all of our traveling adventures, the three of us grew even closer as a family. Rod took us to New York City and Chicago for long weekends in the winter. We also went to the little condo we purchased in Canmore, Alberta, every summer. For two weeks, the boys would play a couple of rounds of golf while I had spa treatments. Rod and I would go by ourselves in the fall. We hiked the beautiful Rocky Mountain trails and went fly fishing. We ate at our newfound favorite restaurants, either in Canmore, Banff, or Lake Louise.

As I watched the sunrises and sunsets each day, I longed to feel all of them: Billy, Mom, Stormy, and Grandpa—all of them with me. I knew in my heart that they were there beside me. I felt so much love and light.

Do not be afraid, little flock, for your Father is pleased to give you the Kingdom.

—LUKE 12:32

CHAPTER 21

Suddenly a great army of heaven's angels appeared
with the angel, singing praises to God:
"Glory to God in the highest heaven, and peace
on earth to those with whom he is pleased!"

—Luke 2:13-1

Some years later, Rod and I took our boat out and brought our two-year-old white Golden Retriever Coby with us for the first time. As usual, I synced the music to my phone and turned on the shuffle button. I love listening to my music all of the time, but especially when we are out boating. It is so comforting to me.

We were anxious to see how Coby would do on the boat. We didn't want him to jump overboard, so I stayed by his side, holding him as we pulled out of the boat dock, through the back waterways out towards the Gulf of Mexico. It was a beautiful day, around 84 degrees with various little fluffy white clouds in the blue sky. Coby and I sat in the front of the boat with the wind in our face and the sun on our backs.

My hair whipped and blew wild all around me, but it felt really good. Various songs played in the background. As I closed my eyes and held onto Coby, I suddenly felt like a little girl again with my dog. My mind drifted back to when I was little, and I could actually feel "her" again—the sweet, innocent little girl who always smelled of outdoors and dogs; who never truly knew the love of her real father, but was lucky enough to know the true love of a stepfather. A little girl who adored her mother and sisters with all of her heart and just wanted to love and protect them. A girl who didn't understand why she had to run over her dog, but now felt that dog right beside her somehow. A young woman who had given up on life, but fought the circumstances around her, which made her stronger and more empowered, and now, she cherished every day.

I opened my eyes and watched the sun dance like diamonds on the turquoise water. "Roll Me Away" by Bob Seeger came on and my eyes teared up, but not with tears of sorrow or grief. I shed tears of joy. Joy because I knew they are all with me—Billy, Mom, Stormy,

Coby and me on our boat, 2017

Grandpa, Steph, and Gram,* and even my little baby Bella that I lost. I feel them: when I find a feather from Billy; in a butterfly that dances around me; in a song; in my garden around all of my flowers; when I feel a little tingle on my skin. They are all around me.

    I felt my heart beating, and for the first time in my life, I felt complete peace. I took back my arm that had been wrapped around Coby and ran my fingers through my hair. Tangled light-brown tresses were caught in my fingers and wedding ring. I brought my hand up to see how many hairs I had lost and noticed that the sunlight had turned the light-brown hairs to a golden hue. Then, I released them, along with all of my grief, to the wind.

---

* See Epilogue.

"Light of Day"

By Beau for his writing class at college
September, 2017

She can't stand the person she sees in the mirror
Her face once beamed with happiness and joy
Now a shadow of a face she once saw clearer
Her voice lost upon people who choose not to hear her
And play with her emotions for their own ploy.
All she can see are the scars of her past
She fears will never go away
Her memories are shadows that have long been cast
As scars they will forever last
While thoughts make her contemplate her life today
But today she woke up with a reason to smile
Jumped out of her bed and saw the light of day
She felt she could see for miles, miles, and miles
Her life had a purpose and was worthwhile
And it no longer mattered what anyone had to say
She met a guy who was kind and treated her right
They started a family and lived a happy life
She now wears her scars in clear sight
Her past demons defeated, she won the fight
Gone was the pain that used to cut like a knife.

May the grace of our Lord Jesus Christ be with you all.

—2 THESSALONIANS 3:18

EPILOGUE

Praise God, from whom all blessings flow;
Praise Him, all creatures here below;
Praise Him above, ye heavenly host;
Praise Father, Son, and Holy Ghost. Amen.

—The Doxology

My sweet Gram left this world quietly, in her sleep just as she had wanted, in the summer of 2015, at almost 101. At her service, I read the following parable sent to me by a friend when my mom passed. I have carried it in my purse ever since.

When I read it, as I do often, I feel Mom with me. I dedicated it to Mom and Gram as well as all of the "moms" in our family.

A Little Parable for Mothers
By Temple Bailey

The young mother set her foot on the path of life. "Is the way long?" she asked.

And her guide said: "Yes, And the way is hard. And you will be old before you reach the end of it. But the end will be better than the beginning."

But the young mother was happy, and she would not believe that anything could be better than these years. So, she played with her children, and gathered flowers for them along the way, and bathed with them in the clear streams; and the sun shone on them, and life was good, and the young mother cried, "Nothing will ever be lovelier than this."

Then night came, and storm, and the path was dark, and the children shook with fear and cold, and the mother drew them close and covered them with her mantle, and the children said, "Oh, we are not afraid, for you are near, and no harm can come," and the mother said, "This is better than the brightness of day, for I have taught my children courage."

And the morning came, and there was a hill ahead, and the children climbed and grew weary, and the mother was weary, but at all times she said to her children, "A little patience, and we are there." So the children climbed, and when they reached the top, they said, "We could not have done it without you, mother."

And the mother, when she lay down that night, looked up at the stars, and said, "This is a better day than the last, for my children have learned fortitude in the face of hardness. Yesterday I gave them courage. Today I have given them strength."

And the next day came strange clouds which darkened the earth—clouds of war and hate and evil, and the children groped and stumbled, and the mother said: "Look up, lift your eyes to the light." And the children looked and saw above the clouds an everlasting Glory, and it guided them and brought them beyond the darkness. And that night the mother said, "This is the best day of all, for I have shown my children God."

And the days went on, and the weeks and the months and the years, and the mother grew old, and she was little and bent. But her children were tall and strong, and walked with courage. And when the way was rough, they lifted her, for she was as light as a feather; and at last they came to a hill, and beyond the hill they could see a shining road and golden gates flung wide. And the mother said: "I have reached the end of my journey. And now I know that the end is better than the beginning, for my children can walk alone, and their children after them."

And the children said, "You will always walk with us, mother, even when you have gone through the gates." And they stood and watched her as she went on alone, and the gates closed after her. And they said: "We cannot see her, but she is with us still. A mother like ours is more than a memory. She is a living Presence."

That story reminds me so much of both Mom and Gram. Both are a living presence in my life.

* * *

I believe in God, the Father almighty, creator of heaven and earth.
I believe in Jesus Christ, God's only Son, our Lord, who was conceived by the Holy Spirit, born of the Virgin Mary, suffered under Pontius Pilate, was crucified, died, and was buried; he descended to the dead.
On the third day he rose again; he ascended into heaven, he is seated at the right hand of the Father, and he will come to judge the living and the dead.
I believe in the Holy Spirit, the holy catholic Church, the communion of saints, the forgiveness of sins, the resurrection of the body, and the life everlasting.
Amen.

—APOSTLES' CREED

My sweet younger sister Steph passed away in early 2017. She was just 46 years old.

We were as close as Stormy and I had been, especially after Stormy's accident. Like with Mom, Steph and I used to talk on the phone daily. But she started drinking heavily after Mom passed. We all pleaded with her to get help, to try to overcome it, at least for her daughters. She tried rehab twice, but after some time, she would sink back into her old habits. She stopped calling me and would not take my calls. When she did and I tried to talk to her, she would hang up on me. We went weeks, then eventually months, without talking.

The disease progressively got worse and eventually overtook her. She was never the same after Mom passed and couldn't cope with life without her, even though her four beautiful daughters needed her. God bless her; she was just heartbroken. My nieces are coping as can be expected and are well cared for by my brother-in-law as well as our extended family members.

Later in 2017, Rod had a heart attack. I took him to the hospital after he told me his chest didn't feel right. He had had bypass surgery on five arteries 17 years before and was monitored every six months, so this was completely unexpected. The heart attack itself happened after we got to the hospital and he was admitted, which was a good thing.

I was so scared of losing him. I prayed, asking God, "Please don't take him, too!" Rod has been the light of my life and the reason I have been able to endure the last years. The doctor said his arteries were 90% blocked but that he could not put stents in. Another open-heart surgery would eventually be needed, but not right away. They modified his medicines and ordered him to exercise, and now Rod tells me he feels great. I feel like I am walking on eggshells, though. It's difficult not to give into the fear of losing him, but I am trying with my faith in God's plan.

I remind myself to cherish every moment we have. Rod has been my angel, my soulmate, my rock, and the wellspring of strength that keeps me going. I tell myself that I have to hold onto my faith—I will not give into fear. It's a daily struggle. I don't think I could bear losing him. I can hear my mom's sweet voice in my ear, telling me to have faith. For all that Mom had to endure, she never gave up.

Because of Rod, Beau and I have been so blessed, and for this I am so grateful. I thank God every day for both of them, but I also thank God for all of my family including those who are in heaven. My best friend says it amazes her that I can even laugh. I realize I have had to endure many losses, but then I think of how blessed I am to have Rod and my beautiful son Beau to light up my life.

I think I have given up looking for answers about why all these things happened. Maybe that is a good thing. Somehow I'm sure that it is all going according to God's plan. Someday, when I get "home," I will see his intricate, beautiful plan that was not only my life, but the lives of my family and how we all intertwined with each other—how we all supported and aided in each of our "promises" to God, each other, and ourselves in this life. I feel it in the depth of my soul that this is true. I don't know what the future holds, but whatever his plan is, I have made a promise that I will try to keep.

I'm trying to hold onto the good, Mom.

Then I saw a new heaven and a new earth. The first heaven and the first earth disappeared, and the sea vanished. And I saw the Holy City, the new Jerusalem, coming down out of heaven from God, prepared and ready, like a bride dressed to meet her husband. I heard a loud voice speaking from the throne: "Now God's home is with mankind! He will live with them, and they shall be his people. God himself will be with them, and he will be their God. He will wipe away all tears from their eyes. There will be no more death, no more grief or crying or pain. The old things have disappeared."

—REVELATION 21:1–4

www.ingramcontent.com/pod-product-compliance
Lightning Source LLC
Chambersburg PA
CBHW071357290426
44108CB00014B/1591